ICT Use in Indian Education

ICT Use in Indian Education

P. Satyanarayana
Laksmi Mantha
C. Sesharatnam

(2024, First Published in 2020)

Rs. 995, US$ 40

ISBN: 978-93-88691-39-0

2026 PoD Impression

ICT Use in Indian Education

Published by:
SHIPRA PUBLICATIONS
LG 18-19, Pankaj Central Market
I.P. Ext., Patparganj, Delhi 110092, India
91 11 47322068; 9650028065, 9810522367
info@shiprapublication.com
www.shiprapublication.com

Contents

1
Technology and Education

Technology is the collection of techniques, skills, methods, and processes used in the production of goods or services or in the accomplishment of objectives, such as scientific investigation. Technology can be the knowledge of techniques, processes, and the like, or it can be embedded in machines to allow for operation without detailed knowledge of their workings. Systems (e.g. machines) applying technology by taking an input, changing it according to the system's use, and then producing an outcome are referred to as technology systems or technological systems.

The simplest form of technology is the development and use of basic tools. The prehistoric discovery of how to control fire and the later Neolithic Revolution increased the available sources of food, and the invention of the wheel helped humans to travel in and control their environment. Developments in historic times, including the printing press, the telephone, and the Internet, have lessened physical barriers to communication and allowed humans to interact freely on a global scale.

Technology has many effects. It has helped develop more advanced economies (including today's global economy) and has allowed the rise of a leisure class. Many technological processes produce unwanted by-products known as pollution and deplete natural resources to the detriment of Earth's environment. Innovations have always influenced the values of a society and raised new questions in the ethics of technology. Examples include the rise of the notion of efficiency in terms of human productivity, and the challenges of bioethics.

Philosophical debates have arisen over the use of technology, with disagreements over whether technology improves the human condition or worsens it. Neo-Luddism, anarcho-primitivism, and similar reactionary movements criticize the pervasiveness of technology, arguing that it harms the environment and alienates people; proponents of ideologies, such as transhumanism and techno-progressivism view continued technological progress as beneficial to society and the human condition.

One of the defining features of development today is the relationship between education and technology, stimulated by the spectacular growth in internet connectivity and mobile penetration. We live in a connected world. An estimated

40 per cent of the world's population now uses the internet and this number is growing at a remarkable rate. While there are significant variations in internet connectivity among countries and regions, the number of households with such links in the global South has now overtaken those in the global North. Moreover, over 70 per cent of mobile telephone subscriptions worldwide are now in the global South. Five billion people are expected to go from no to full connectivity within the next twenty years. However, there are still significant gaps among countries and regions, for example, between urban and rural areas. Limited broadband speed and lack of connectivity hamper access to knowledge, participation in society and economic developments.

The internet has transformed how people access information and knowledge, how they interact, and the direction of public management and business. Digital connectivity holds promise for gains in health, education, communication, leisure and well-being. Artificial intelligence advances, 3D printers, holographic recreation, instant transcription, voice-recognition and gesture-recognition software are only some examples of what is being tested. Digital technologies are re-shaping human activity from daily life to international relations, from work to leisure, re-defining multiple aspects of our private and public life.

Such technologies have expanded opportunities for freedom of expression and for social, civic and political mobilization, but they also raise important concerns. The availability of personal information in the cyber world, for example, brings up significant issues of privacy and security. New spaces for communication and socialization are transforming what constitutes the idea of 'social' and they require enforceable legal and other safeguards to prevent their overuse, abuse and misuse. Examples of such misuse of the internet, mobile technology and social media range from cyber-bullying to criminal activity, even to terrorism. In this new cyber world, educators need to better prepare new generations of 'digital natives' to deal with the ethical and social dimensions of not only existing digital technologies but also those yet to be invented.

Technology plays an increasingly significant role in improving access to education for people living in impoverished areas and developing countries. Educational technology is not merely a matter of education and technology alone but is also about the societal culture, wherein that educational technology is implemented.

The OLPC foundation, a group out of MIT Media Lab and supported by several major corporations, has a stated mission to develop a $100 laptop for delivering educational software. They are sold at cost or given away based on donations.

In Africa, the New Partnership for Africa's Development (NEPAD) has launched an "e-school programme" to provide all 600,000 primary and high schools with computer equipment, learning materials and internet access within 10 years. An International Development Agency project called nabuur.com, started with the support of former American President Bill Clinton, uses the Internet to allow co-operation by individuals on issues of social development.

India is developing technologies that will bypass land-based telephone and Internet infrastructure to deliver distance learning directly to its students. In 2004, the Indian Space Research Organisation launched EDUSAT, a communications satellite providing access to educational materials that can reach more of the country's population at a greatly reduced cost.

An AI-based tutoring system, Education Dominance, was put into an entry-level IT school in Pensacola by the US. Navy. This system relates to a human tutor in which the student's progress is monitored while providing individual assessments. According to the Navy, the students that worked with the digital tutoring system consistently performed better on the tests than did the students who did not use the digital tutor. The adaptive technology appears to affect students positively because it can assist individuals that have different learning skills than others and there for better equipped to learn on their own.

Dictionaries and scholars have offered a variety of definitions. The *Merriam-Webster Learner's Dictionary* offers a definition of the term: "the use of science in industry, engineering, etc., to invent useful things or to solve problems" and "a machine, piece of equipment, method, etc. that is created by technology" Ursula Franklin, in her 1989 "Real World of Technology" lecture, gave another definition of the concept; it is practice, the way we do things around here. The term is often used to imply a specific field of technology, or to refer to high technology or just consumer electronics, rather than technology as a whole. Bernard Stiegler, in *Technics and Time,* 1, defines technology in two ways: as the pursuit of life by means other than life, and as organized inorganic matter.

Importance of Technology in Education

Ten reasons for the importance of technology in education are:

- Students demand it.
- New teachers demand it.
- Kids are the digital native.
- Kids can learn at their own pace.
- With technology, there are no limitations.
- Technology has the ability to enhance relationships between teachers and students.
- Testing has gone online.
- Multitude of resources.
- Technology keeps kids engaged.
- Technology is necessary outside of primary and secondary education.

Potential of Technology for Improving Education

- Better Simulation and Models

- Global Learning
- Virtual Manipulatives
- Probes and Sensors
- More Efficient Assessment
- Story-telling and Multimedia
- E-books
- Epistemic Games

Benefits of Technology in Education

One of the benefits of technology in education is that it increases the reach of educational programmes in the society. Under the traditional setting, individuals must access institutions that offer learning programmes for them to get an education.

The existence of formal frameworks means that only a few numbers of individuals can access formal educational programmes at any given time.

With the rise of innovative ways of using technology in education, many people can now easily access learning programmes.

The rise in the use of technology in education has made learning very accessible. An educational technologist can now easily package content in the form of tutorial videos, audio files, and even textual documents.

Technology is revolutionizing the entire education sector. The revolution can see in the emergence and growth of changes in the teaching and learning process.

Improvement of Learning

The following are ways that technology could be better leveraged to improve learning:

- With the widespread availability of student databases that are able to track individual progress, teachers are encouraged to identify learning objectives and differentiate instructions based on the needs of their students.
- Whatever teachers attempt to present instruction using technology they should do so using a channel that is relevant to the objectives, the learning style, mode and the technology selected.
- When evaluating technology based instruction, there needs to be appropriate evaluation techniques that are in line with the methods of instruction, objectives and the technology.
- Teachers can design follow-up activities when using technology to evaluate students' learning and the role technology played in that process.

Overall technology is central to many sectors of society and its integration into the education process has great promise for student learning. With technology, one can expect increased efficiency and effectiveness on both the part of teachers and students. Technology can also prompt pedagogical change and address issues that affect learning, teaching and social organizations. Technology cab, therefore, be seen as both a tool and a catalyst for change. Students should embrace technology for them to benefit and teachers should be open to introducing technology into the classroom to improve and innovate their teaching practice.

Potential of Technology in Promoting Literacy

- Enhanced learning
- Broadening access to literacy education
- Creating local content
- Professional development of teachers
- Cultivating a literacy conducive environment

Challenges of Technologies in Education

Despite early implementation of technologies in education system, India still faces teething problem for the new technologies in education. Some of them are:

- Not enough or limited access to computer hardware & computer software in education institutes. This not only aids in visual learning, but also it is interactive so that students can draw, write, or manipulate images on the interactive whiteboard.
- Digital video eliminates the need for in classroom hardware and allows teachers and students to access video clips immediately by not utilizing the public internet.
- Streamed video websites can be utilized to enhance a classroom lesson.
- Tools that motivate studying by making studying more fun or individualised for the student.
- The field of educational games and serious games has been growing significantly over the last few years. The digital games are being provided as tools for the classroom and have a lot of positive feedback including higher motivation for students.
- There are many other tools being utilized depending on the local school board and funds available at their disposal.

Twenty Technology Skills Every Education Should Have

1. Word processing skill
2. Spreadsheet skill
3. Data base skill
4. Electronic presentation skill
5. Web navigation
6. Website design skill
7. E-mail management skill
8. Digital camera

9. Computer network Knowledge application to school system
10. Fire management & window explorer skill
11. Downloading software from the web
12. Installing computer software onto a computer system
13. Web CT or black board teaching skill
14. Video conferring skill
15. Computer related software devices
16. Scanner knowledge
17. Knowledge of PDAs
18. Deep web knowledge
19. Education copyright knowledge
20. Computer security knowledge

2
Technology in Indian Education

India is known as one of the world's top education destinations in the global education. With some of the best universities and colleges, India has been successful in attracting bright talents all over the world. Indian education system is robust and built on strong foundations, according to Indian Brand Equity Foundation, Indian education market is currently pegged at $ 100 billion with higher education contributing to 59.7 per cent, school education at 38.1 per cent, pre-school at 1.6 per cent and the remainder 0.6 per cent consists of technology and multi-media based education.

India is not be the early adopter of technology in the education sector but with access to high speed broadband internet and low lost computers and mobile devices, there has been growth in the use of technology for learning. Today, India is one of the fastest growing markets for e-learning based products and services. There are different ways technology can be used to bring about reformation in the Indian education system. Even government aims to increase digital literacy of the country to 50 per cent from current 15 per cent by bringing out favourable policies to give impetus to technology based learning. Many entrepreneurs and startups have grabbed this opportunity to develop technology based educational products for private and government based schools, colleges and universities.

Uses of Technology in the Education Sector

1. *Distance education:* Distance education is a way of learning where the students or working professionals can learn the courses remotely through online access and interact with faculty via online classroom. It helps students to interact with their mentors or tutors directly through chat, e-mail or phone call. Indian is a developing country and for many students who are living in remote places or villages getting degree for higher education is still a distant dream. In such instances technology enabled distance education can help them to complete their studies, upgrade their skills and get degrees. This gives the students or working professionals the flexibility to learn at their own time without the compulsion of going to classes.

According to a Report released by All India Survey on Higher Education 2014-2015 by Ministry of Human Resource Development, the total enrolment of students for Distance education constitute 11.7 per cent out of which 46 per cent are female students. Availability of broadband and hi-speed internet along with low cost computers to tier 2 and tier 3 cities has made learning seamless without any glitches.

2. *Classroom based learning:* Now-a-days technology has become integral part of classroom based teaching. Today in many schools, colleges and universities in India instead of blackboard/projector screens are used for teaching. Hand writings of teachers are replaced by power point presentation. Students experience a different kind of set up in today's technology based classroom. Gadgets like tablets and laptops are used to take down notes.

3. *Online learning management system:* Many colleges and universities in India are integrating online Learning Management System or LMS platform into their web portal. Students can remotely login to access course material and also attend live classes with teachers.

Pre-recorded lectures, videos can be uploaded on the LMS platform making it easy for students to go through it multiple times. LMS adoption is still poor in many parts of India where students do not have the access to computers or broadband internet. However, government is providing computers to remote areas and creating content that consumes less data and can be easily accessed on internet.

4. *Learning through mobile apps:* India has become the second biggest smart phone market in the world after China with more than 220 million active users. This presents a huge opportunity for delivering e-learning content through mobile apps. Today, educational mobile apps are available on popular platforms like Android and iOS. Developers are creating educational apps based on particular subjects. They are simplifying complex concepts with easy to understand illustrations and animations, puzzles, games, etc.

There are also certain websites like Khan Academy and various YouTube channels that offer video lectures by eminent scholars and teachers in various subjects.

Even though some of the educational institutions in India ranks on par with world's best universities and colleges, the use of technology is still limited in Indian education sector. With the rising cost of education, technology based learning can come to the rescue of those who wants to go for higher degree but cannot afford it. Government needs to play an active role in encouraging educational institution in adopting latest technology for teachings and delivering course content. With its population of 1.2 billion people the scope for technology based learning can surpass that of many developed and developing nations.

EduTech is the Future

The advent of internet has shrunk the entire world into a global village. With everything available digitally, it is very easy for a person from Patna to know the latest research being conducted at Columbia University. Also, PM Narendra Modi's digitization initiative and even demonetization has paved the way for the growth of digital education medium in the country.

In the past, education system in India, was restricted to the archaic simple classrooms with blackboards and quarterly exams to measure the students' progress. But all that has changed in the past couple of years with the internet boom, at least in cities. Today, India ranks second only to China with 348 million internet users which is expected to reach about 555.3 million users by 2021. This exploration of technology has further led to the influx and rise of EdTech companies in India. These firms brought the fun back into learning through their innovative concepts and novel teaching methods.

The availability of low cost and high-speed internet has made it possible for EdTech to reach a wider and vast section of the Indian population. While there are many remote parts in India where students still have to travel for an hour or more to reach their schools/colleges, EdTech has brought classroom into one's living room. An online classroom is not restricted by location or geography and has removed all boundaries imposed by the traditional education system. In the past when one missed a school/college lecture, it was difficult to catch up with the syllabus. But now through online tutoring it is possible to not only catch up with studies but even stay ahead of the game.

Moreover, as the entire nation is shifting towards digitization where people are encouraged to pay their milk vendor through Paytm, learning through technology has become more easy and interactive. Learning through TataSky or online tutors has become simpler in this fast-moving world where everything is so competitive and chaotic. In cities like Delhi, where there is a huge traffic problem and going from place to another consumes majority time, an online class helps you save valuable time. With the help of EdTech mediums, one can learn from the comfort of their home, rather than spending hours in commute from one location to another. This precious time can further be used productively to sharpen their skills.

EdTech offers teachers/educational institutions practical and smart ways to evaluate a student's progress. Rather than waiting for quarterly exam results to know a student's progress in a subject one can use EdTech tools to monitor their performance daily. It offers you ways to track a student's performance by going through his scores, classroom attendance, participation and then come up with a plan to work on the weak areas.

EduTech is the Future of Indian Education

Unlike the limited knowledge offered by boring textbooks, EdTech offers you a plethora of options to learn. This combined with easy availability of smart phones and internet has given students an option to grasp concepts which were earlier learnt through traditional method. Since all students don't have the same learning capability, one can personalize these EdTech tools accordingly one's needs. A student can learn through concepts taught by Byjus, Khan Academy or opt for online tutoring provided by GuruQ.

EdTech offers parents and children a stress-free environment to learn subjects and upgrade their knowledge. In a changing world India needs to move towards technology because that is the way forward.

Technology is the Way Forward for Indian Education

India's education system is in a crisis. It is a crisis that technology can play a critical role in solving. The 2014 Annual Status of Education Report (ASER) showed that nearly 75 per cent children in Class V cannot solve a Class III division problem. Alongside low student learning levels, such as these, India also faces a shortage of 1.4 million teachers—meaning many children face even more difficult access to quality instruction.

So, what can be done? One piece of the puzzle is to think about what types of learning can be made available through technology that can both help augment a child's experience in a classroom and also give access to those in rural areas.

EdTech allows students to study at their own pace, which means that gaps in learning are addressed quickly and easily. Self-learning models enable anywhere, anytime learning by reaching directly to students.

The power of technology can also connect students to high-quality resources, regardless of their location. Personalised learning using adaptive tools and allowing teachers to differentiate instruction to meet varying student interests is the best way to think of the classroom of the future.

EdTech can help to promote higher order skills, such as critical thinking, problem solving and creativity by encouraging students to participate in project-based work and allowing teachers the time to engage actively with students in such areas. When class time is freed up by using technology, teachers are enabled to spend it with students or in small group work situations, enabling learning in many different ways. This can be achieved through blended learning models that combine one-to-one learning on computers with teacher instruction. The Nalanda project by the Motivation for Excellence Foundation in Mumbai explores the potential of learning mathematics using a blend of teacher instruction and self-learning through an offline digital learning tool.

We need to recognise that the large number of low-income children in the Indian education system calls for the creation of open educational resources that can be made available free or at a low cost to the students. The cost of proprietary digital content, ranging from Rs. 1,000 to Rs. 2,000 per year per subject, is often too high for students, whether they're studying in government or private schools. Moreover, we need to create products in local languages that cater to students studying in vernacular medium schools, especially to first generation learners.

With the Internet and mobile infrastructure becoming widely available, the government pushing for the adoption of digital technology, and entrepreneurs and funders collaborating to create innovative solutions, there is tremendous potential for technology to continue to improve the quality of education and student learning levels in India. This is a special time in history, when we actually have a chance to help all our students have access to world-class education.

ICT has changed the face of education over the last few decades. "It has proved to be a boon to both the teachers and the learners. Looking for matter beyond the textbooks is no longer a challenge with respect to time and resources anymore."

Assisting in the growth of ICT learning in the country, several brands are ensuring to create options for educational institutions.

Recognising the importance of digital literacy in rural India, in 2013 Samsung India launched a Smart Class initiative in collaboration with Navodaya Vidyalaya Samiti. The initiative is available across 500 Jawahar Navodaya Vidyalaya Schools, benefitting over 2.5 lakh students. The brand has imparted training to over 8,000 teachers on interacting technology.

Gopal Singh Tomar, Principal, Jawahar Navodaya Vidyalaya, Dadri (Uttar Pradesh) feels "60 per cent of the students in our school are the first time users of technology or Smart Class".

Stating that students are now confident and the use of technology is helping our teaching also to a great extent, he said: "Our results have improvement post-ICT."

"Smart Classes have helped one of our students Akash Karan in developing a mobile application. This app helps the user in calling his/her dear and near ones in case of any emergency just by using the app and that too by a single touch."

Technology is Evolving

Indian education system is evolving in many ways, owing to the advancement of technology as well as rapid change of mentality of the people of all segment of society. Government intervention in merging technology with pedagogy system of education has taken Indian education to a new avenue, opening new doors of opportunities for both the educator as well as student.

There are two segments in every education system, teacher and learner. In a traditional education system, the teacher narrates a topic to students, holds demonstration of the topic occasionally, and then assessed the students. However, not every student has the same grasping capabilities, due to which traditional models of education are gradually paving way for newer innovative methods supported by technology. Govt. of India has acknowledged the limitations of existing pedagogy system and take initiative of incorporating ICT in the education system.

With the help of ICT, teachers can easily explain the complex situations to the student and the student, too, retains information better, remembering the visual explanation of a particular situation for a longer time.

India is emerging as a superpower and it cannot function without the support of ICT. The gap between demand and supply of higher education has urged the government and institutions of the country to formulate policies and initiatives so that education can easily integrate with ICT.

The central and state governments have taken various initiatives for integration of ICT with education system. Since the past two to three decades, the Indian education system has been plagued by many challenges, such as lack of students, poor infrastructure, lack of quality teacher, and a standard curriculum, to name a few. With the integration of ICT in schools, education in India is poised for a paradigm shift, where the education system will be compatible with international education standard.

However, there are many hurdles for its successful integration. ICT requires internet, computer based infrastructure and also satellite support and the process of installation is expensive. Moreover, teachers need to be efficiently trained to understand ICT and how they can utilise its numerous benefits best to successfully impart knowledge to the students.

In the current digital day and age, it is imperative that schools and institutes integrate ICT and be attuned to the modern needs and requirement of students. The use of ICT in learning not only results in the cognitive, social and emotional development of a child, but also has a major motivational influence on his/her learning capabilities.

IT and ICT Initiatives by Indian Government

1. National Digital Literary Mission
2. Vidyanjali
3. Bharatavani
    - Paathyapustaka Kosh
    - Jnana Kosh
    - Shabda Kosh
    - Bhasha Kosh
    - Suchanaa Pradyogikii Kosh
    - Bahamaadhyama Kosh
4. Web Based School GIS
5. Sarva Shiksha Abhiyan
6. Rashtriya Madhyamik Shiksha Abhiyan
7. Shala Darpan
8. e-pathshala
9. Swayam
10. Image Courtesy
11. Experimental Learning
12. Infolding Multiple Intelligences in the Classroom
13. Integrity and Ethics
14. Early Childhood Care & Education
15. Creating the Happiest Learning Spaces
16. Early Childhood Development Milestones
17. Read Aloud
18. Dance their way to a Fitter India

19. New ways to teach Science in the Early Childhood Classroom
20. A Global Idea of Montessori

Technology in Schools

The Information and Communication Technology (ICT) in schools have been subsumed in the Rashtriya Madhyamik Shiksha Abhiyan (RMSA). Now ICT in schools is a component of the RMSA. The Information and Communication Technology (ICT) in schools was launched in December, 2004 and revised in 2010 to provide opportunities to secondary stage students to mainly build their capacity on ICT skills and make them learn through computer aided learning process. The Scheme is a major catalyst to bridge the digital divide amongst students of various socio-economic and other geographical barriers. The Scheme provides support to States/UTs to establish computer labs on sustainable basis.

The scheme has essentially four components:

- The first one is the partnership with State Government and Union Territories Administrations for providing computer aided education to Secondary and Higher Secondary Government and Government aided schools.
- The second is the establishment of smart schools, which shall be technology demonstrators.
- The third component is teacher related interventions, such as provision for engagement of an exclusive teacher, capacity enhancement of all teachers in ICT and a scheme for national ICT award as a means of motivation.
- Fourth one relates to the development of an e-content, mainly through Central Institute of Education Technologies (CIET), six State Institutes of Education Technologies (SIETs) and 5 Regional Institutes of Education (RIEs), as also through outsourcing.

The scheme currently covers both Government and Government aided Secondary and Higher Secondary Schools. Financial assistance is provided for procurement of computers and peripherals, educational software, training of teachers, development of e-contents, Internet connectivity & set up of smart schools. So far, 87033 government and government aided secondary and higher secondary schools have been approved for coverage under ICT in Schools Scheme.

Government of India Support to ICT in Education

Worldwide research has shown that ICT can lead to improved student learning and better teaching methods. A report made by the National Institute of Multimedia Education in Japan, proved that an increase in student exposure to educational ICT through curriculum integration has a significant and positive impact on student achievement, especially in terms of "Knowledge Comprehension" · "Practical skill" and "Presentation skill" in subject areas, such as mathematics, science, and social study.

In India, students strength is increasing day by day due to growth of population, awareness about advantages of education and govt. policies & facilities to promote education. Indian govt. is providing free education, free books, free dress, free mid-day meal and scholarship, etc. It is not easy to do all these because of geographical structure, infrastructure and economic problem of country. ICT can play an important roll in achieving them them.

India has the third largest system of education in the world, next only to USA and China, with more than 700 universities and around 30000 colleges. To introduce ICT-enabled education in such a large system one needs to have high quality multi-media enriched content in different disciplines for various courses including its multi-lingual conversion, capacity building of teachers and students in ICT skills and state-of-the-art infrastructure along with networking and internet connectivity via Virtual Private Network (VPN)/broadband connectivity for disseminating the content and affordable access devices so that it reaches the doorsteps of the learners. The ongoing National Mission on Education through ICT (NMEICT) is a major initiative of the Govt. of India in this direction with an aim to leverage the potential of ICT in providing high quality personalized and interactive content, free of cost, to all the learners.

In order to use technology to help achieve the goals of education in a better and more effective way, one has to be first of all clear about what our expectations are from the education system, what and how do we want our students to learn and what type of individuals our classrooms should produce-rote learners or those with an analytical mind having an in-depth understanding of the subject?

Some Barriers in Technology Use

Avoiding nature of people: In general, the attitude of people is not of acceptance of ICT. People are ignoring the importance and need of ICT. When peoples are having problems with themselves mentally or technically, they put the blame on technology.

People think technology means solution for all problems in magic way, which is not practically possible. People have to develop themselves also.

Economic problems: Developing countries like INDIA and other Asian countries have financial problems also. Economic positions of common people are not good, so it is difficult to afford for computer, tab, and android phone.

Lack of good quality infra support: In developing countries like INDIA, electricity, network, and other facilities are not available. People are not getting proper power supply, if they are getting that not in proper standard. Same is with the network, telecommunication companies are just making money not providing proper network.

Gadgets maintenance problems: In developing countries, all gadgets like laptop, tab, and android mobile have the maintenance problems. Technology is changing very fast, next morning we can see new model in market, and there is no service facilities for old models. Govt. don't have any clear cut policy on service part or customers education for proper use of gadgets.

Social and culture scenario: Social and culture structure of INDIA and Asian countries is different from western culture. Using technology among the common people is not easily acceptable. Society raises the voice even against the use of mobile by girls.

Browsing internet is not safe, this is one of the reason that society is concern with cultural and social loss of children. It is very difficult to safeguard the children from porn sites.

Computer skill and English language problem: Even now a day s computer and English is not common among the common peoples in INDIA. Still 70 per cent of rural schools don't have facility of computer and English is also a problem to students, and both are necessary for education with ICT.

Initiatives for Quality Improvement

Indian higher education sector is suffering from lack of qualified faculties even in premier institutes like IITs and NITs. Therefore, Indian ministries and premier education institutions have taken many ICT (Information and Communication Technology) based initiatives to improve access to quality education by every individual of India sitting anywhere between Kashmir to Kanyakumari. Article highlights major ICT based programmes started recently in India.

In order to improve GER in higher education by 5 percentage during 11th five-year plan, Indian Government commenced the NME-ICT project and allotted a budget of INR 5 billion. The major focus of this scheme was to fulfill three key cardinal principles of education policy viz., access, equity, and quality. Therefore, the project targeted to provide high bandwidth availability with low-cost computing devices (Aakash tablet) to most of the institutes in a phase-wise manner. Another major goal of the project was to generate good quality study material and relevant contents. Some of the key objectives of the mission are as follows:

- Effective utilization of intellectual resources and anytime availability of desired knowledge at appropriate levels to self-paced learners.
- Platform for sharing ideas, techniques, and knowledge resources to support learner and scholars.
- Utilize the full potential of developments in the field of ICT to take the resources at the door step of the learner.
- Emphasis on e-learning, content generation, evaluation, and mentoring.
- Develop a repository of e-books, e-generals and provide easy access to the learners.
- Encourage teachers to participate in the digital era of learning and be available on the internet to guide learners.
- Foster multi-lingual content generation for the diversified Indian population and motivate indigenous Open Source Software development.

- Utilization of satellites to broadcast study channels via Direct to Home (DTH) service.
- Online certification based courses for self-paced learners by reputed institutes of India.

Under the banner of NME-ICT, a project called National Programme on Technology Enhanced Learning (NPTEL) like Massachusetts Institute of Technology's Open Courseware is started to provide video lectures of well-known professors of Indian Institute of Technologies (IITs) and Indian Institute of Science (IISs) in almost all the engineering courses. Presently NPTEL provides India's largest repository of free video lectures for engineering students with certification facility after course completion.

IIT, Kharagpur and IIT, Bombay together working on a project called T10K10 (Train 10 Thousand Teachers). It is a major initiative under the NME-ICT to improve the teaching skill of engineering college teachers of the country in core Engineering and Science subjects. IIT, Madras started Quality Enhancement in Engineering Education (QEEE) that offers live classes and virtual lab environment as a supplement material to the colleges lacking basic pedagogical resources viz. qualified teachers, well-equipped labs, and quality content. Under NME-ICT project, IIT, Bombay started spoken tutorial programme that provides audio-video tutorial of only open source software in various Indian regional languages. IIT, Bombay also executed the project of India's first low-cost tablet named 'Aakash' and distributed it to around 1,00,000 students at its remote centre. In the future, it is planned to distribute every institute at least a single Aakash tablet.

Other Quality Improvement Initiatives

University Grants Commission of India set up the Consortium for Educational Communication (CEC) as one of the Inter University Centre to cater the needs of Higher Education through the use of Television along with the ICT. Many other initiatives in this connection to use ICT to deliver free, easily accessible and good quality education are also been taken viz. e-PG Pathshala for Post Graduate students, Shiksha for students of Central Board of Secondary Education, E-Gyankosh: a digital content repository, VidyaVahini for school kids, National Digital Library containing 6 million books ranging from primary to PG level, etc.

It is certain that realization of most of the ICT based project is dependent upon good Internet and Wi-Fi connectivity, therefore, Indian HRD ministry recently announced to launch a Campus-Connect programme to make 21,000 colleges and 4,20,000 classrooms Wi-Fi enabled. Under the programme, all the buildings of 700 universities having 1 Gbps bandwidth will be made Wi-Fi enabled.

3
Distance Education

There has been a rapid explosion in the range of technologies now available to education. For over 3,000 years, from Homer, Moses and Socrates onwards, the teacher, in direct, personal contact with the learner, has been the main means of educational communication until the 14th century. When the invention of the printing press facilitated for the first time the large scale spread of knowledge through books and printed materials, however, did not replace the teacher. Teachers retained their role in educational process, since they were needed to help large number of children develop the skills of reading and writing to such an extent that it became necessary to establish educational institution to facilitate greater number of people to be educated.

The industrial networks led for more and more schools and colleges. The introduction of postal service helped the introduction of Correspondence education. Postal service was followed by wireless. It is interesting to recall that the first Director of Education at the BBC thought about the possibility of a 'broadcast university'. The first adult education talk was on 6th October, 1924. The first schools radio programme was broadcasted by the BBC in 1926. Sixteen mm film came into use from the 1930, to be later replaced by to a great extent by television, schools television began in 1957 on a regular scale. Bates records the new technologies in teaching upto1980 and from 1980 as follows:

Upto 1980

Types of Technology

- Teacher
- Book
- Postal Service
- Radio
- Film
- Television

From 1980

Types of Technology

- Audio cassettes
- Audio-conferencing
- Audio-graphic systems
- Video cassettes
- View data/Teletext/Teledom
- Computer based learning
- Laser video discs
- Cable TV
- Satellite TV
- Expert systems
- LCD Projectors
- Search engines
- Mobile Phones
- Wireless networks
- Compact discs
- E-portfolios
- Video cassettes
- Video conferencing
- Electronic mail
- Computer conference
- Internet
- World Wide Web
- Digital video discs
- Fiber optics
- Learning object
- Portals
- Simulations
- Virtual reality

Distance Teaching Universities Use Variety of Technology

Distance teaching universities use a variety of communication technology. The British Open University's charter specifically enjoins it to advance and disseminate learning and knowledge 'by teaching and research by a diversity of means such as broadcasting and technological device appropriate to higher education'. One of the objectives of Indira Gandhi National Open University is "to advance and disseminate learning and knowledge by a diversity of means including the use of any communication technology". In fact, some of the Open universities have titles signifying the influence and importance of communications technology. The prominent examples are: Japan's University of Air and China's Radio and Television Universities. Thus, a notable feature of distance learning system is "the planned use of a wide range of media. suited to the needs of the students". The British Open University was originally conceived as the "University of Air". Technologies can be interactive and non-interactive.

Non-interactive and Interactive Technologies

	Non-interactive	*Interactive*
Audio	• Radio (primary carrier, • Radio (sub-carrier) • Audio tape	• Telephone • Audio teleconferencing
Video	• Open broadcast television • Cable Television (one-way) • Video tape • Instructional television fixed service (ITFS) • Satellite television (one-way) • Slow scan/freeze frame television (one-way)	• Microwave (point to point) • Cable television (Two-way or viewer response) • Show scan/freeze fram television (Two-way) • Electronic blackboard • Satellite television (Two-way) • Video teleconferencing
Computer		• Compute assisted instruction • Computer based instructional management

Radio

The potential advantages of radio for use in learning at a distance programme included "time, cost-effectiveness and localness". While not always essential to most programmes, radio is particularly useful in complementing printed information. Radio can accelerate or extend learning at distance programmes and is useful in reaching isolated rural audiences quickly and relatively inexpensively. While radio programmes are restricted by broadcast time schedules, they are an important component of learning at a distance programmes at the elementary, secondary and post-secondary levels in both industrialized and developing countries.

It was not until the late 1800 that radio became a reality. Ilerts proved the existence of radio-waves in the 1800; less than twenty years later, Marconi transmitted wireless signals across the Atlantic. The invention of the triode vaccum tube amplifier became the "magicLamp" of radio, and with the AC plug-in, radios became a widespread household convenience during the 1920s. After the transistor was invented in 1948, radio became even more widespread. It is now a highly cost-effective way of broadcasting information through out the entire world.

Today, radio can be used (and often is used) to enrich the material delivered to students who are learning at a distance. The popularity, availability, and low cost of radio make it a convenient and practical medium for use in programmes for learning at a distance. Further more, the use of radio can overcome problems associated with illiteracy. However, programmes provided by broadcast radio do have one serious limitations: listeners must be available at the scheduled broadcast hours.

The UK. Open University listed down the following uses of radio:

(i) To provide remedial tutorials, or some other forms of tutorial based feedback.

(ii) To provide corrections, alterations or updating of material, where print re-make budgets are limited, or where print cannot reach students quickly enough.

(iii) To bring to students primary resource material, i.e., recordings which, through careful editing and selection, can demonstrate principles covered in the units. This material may be used in a number of ways, for example:

(a) recordings of naturally occurring events, e.g. political speeches, children talking, concerts or performances, talks previously recorded for other than Open University purposes eyewitness interviews at historical events;

(b) to provide students with a selection of sources of evidence to analyze.

(iv) To bring to student the views and knowledge of eminent people, which can be condensed in an interview, or be edited afterwards, to provide the essential points, which may be more complex or lengthy in written form.

(v) To record especially the voices of people who have not been recorded before, but whose contribution to the course would provide a unique experience (e.g. famous poets reading their own work, civil servants talking-perhaps anonymously-about their role in decision-making).

(vi) To change student attitudes:

(a) by presenting material in a novel manner, or from a non-familiar Viewpoints;

(b) By presenting material in a dramatized form, enabling students to identify with the emotions and viewpoints of the participants.

(vii) To bring alive the performance arts direct into the student's own home, and to demonstrate methods or techniques of drama or music through performance.

(viii) To provide the student with a condensed argument, in letcture form, which may:

(a) reinforce point made elsewhere in the courses.

(b) introduce new concepts not covered elsewhere in the course;

(c) provide an alternative view to that presented in the correspondence text and/or television programmes;

(d) analyze material contained elsewhere in the course; especially in written broadcast notes or television programmes;

(e) summarize the main points of the block or course as far as it has gone, providing integration and orientation;

(f) draw quotations, recorded information, interviews, etc. as evidence in support of (or against) the argument.

(ix) To enable students to perceive the different points of view that exist, and observe ideas being challenged, through discussion and interviews.

In practice, radio never becomes an integrated and essential component in more than a few courses-mainly in the Arts faculty. Even in the early years, when the transmission times used were still convenient for large numbers of students, the average listening rate was not much over 50 per cent; that is, each radio programme was heard, on the average, by little over half of the students for whom it was intended. And as early as1974, it was reported that on the was of OU courses, radio programmes were somewhat peripheral appendices to the printed material.

Television

While radio is generally acceptable, television is not the use of television for education is based on the following reasons:

- Television is no doubt a technologically brilliant medium but it is a format for entertainment, not for education as it is inherently hostile to thought.
- It is in the nature of the medium to trivialize everything it touches and to free the viewer from the obligation to think.
- All ideas are reduced to a lowest common denominator. Television image is one of "low definition" and offers little detail.
- Television suppresses the content of ideas in order to accommodate the requirements or visual intent, i.e. to accommodate the values of show business.
- Television is a low involvement medium; students will be required to do nothing more than watch and television viewing produces an alpha brainwave pattern state (relaxed, inattentive condition).
- Television is synonymous with entertainment and commercials. It is difficult to treat it for serious business.
- Educationists may have brilliant ideas of teaching but they have to accommodate them to television and not vice versa.

The advocates of television for education give the following reasons:

- Electronic communication is a fundamental change on a par with previous great revolutions, such as writing, printing and the telephone and will result in the most far-reaching changes in social progress.
- Many educationists have realized that a piece-meal approach to television results in the waste of a most powerful educational tool. If well used, television is as effective as a good teacher. And if badly used is as ineffective as a bad teacher. At least, both educational institutions and the community, in general, are beginning to awake to the fact that television is not just a trivial and passing phenomenon suitable only for entertainment, but is a medium which could be as significant for

education as is print itself. Further more, the converging technologies of televisions and computing promise even more exciting developments in the future.

- Educational methods must make use of the fact that we remember what we see, more than what we hear-which is one of the most distinguishing features of television.
- The remarks on brainwaves and low involvement are not based on tested generalizations.
- Nor is it correct to make television the scapegoat for any upsurge of violence in a society. The link between television and violence has not been scientifically established.
- Television, in fact, humanizes distance education. The human face on the screen established a rapport and the mass medium in this way really delivers the message on an individual basis.
- Television generates a sense of belonging among the participants of distant education as it enables the sharing of the same programme with thousands of others similarly motivated.
- Most of the criticism of television is in the context of the social situation in the US which need not necessarily happen elsewhere. Not in all countries, for example, do children spend more hours before a television than in school.
- For the educationalist, the debate is really not 'either-or', in other words, the question is not whether television should be used or not as the sole purveyor of lessons; the question is how far television can be used with other media. Television cannot solve all problems.
- It is in the hands of the educationist to ensure that the format does not become more important than the context. Television can, in fact, take over some of the routine tasks and allow more time for profitable interaction with students, when tutors meet them.

The UKOU listed down the following uses of Television:

(i) To demonstrate experiments or experimental situations, particularly:
  - where equipment or phenomena to be observed are large, expensive, inaccessible or difficult to observe without special equipment;
  - where the experimental design is complex;
  - where the measurement of experimental behaviour is not easily reduced to a single scale or dimension (e.g. human behaviour); and
  - where the experimental behaviour may be influenced by uncontrollable but observable variables.

(ii) To bring to students primary resource material, i.e. film or video recordings of actual situations which, through editing and selection, can demonstrate principles covered in the units. This material may be used for a number of purposes, for example:

- film of naturally occurring events (e.g. teaching situations, mental disorders, medical cases) to enable recognition of categories, ˜symptoms, etc;.
- film of naturally occurring events to enable students to analyze situation, using principles or criteria established elsewhere in unit; and
- to provide students with a selection of sources of evidence to analyze; besides contemporary material, it may also include archive film or historical material.

(iii) To record special events, experiments, species, places, people, buildings, etc. which are crucial to the content of units, but may be likely to disappear, die or be destroyed in the near future.

(iv) To bring to students the views or knowledge of eminent people, who are often prepared to be televised but not to write material especially for the institution.

(v) To change student attitudes:

(i) by presenting material in a novel manner, or from an unfamiliar viewpoint;

(ii) by presenting material in a dramatized form, enabling students to identify with the emotions and viewpoints of the main participants; and

(iii) by allowing the students to identify closely with someone in the programme or televised exercise. Who overcomes problems or himself changes his attitudes as a result of evidence presented in the programme.

(iv) To explain or demonstrate activities that the students are to carry out (e.g. home experiments, survey interviewing).

(v) To feedback to students 'mass'or total result of activities or surveys carried out by the students themselves, where the turn around time is too short for printed feedback.

(vi) To illustrate abstract principles involving dynamic change or movements.

(vii) To illustrate abstract principles involving thorough the use of especially constructed physical models.

(viii) To illustrate principles involving two, three or n-dimensional space.

(ix) To use animated, slow-motion, or speeded-up film or videotape to demonstrate changes over time (including computer animation).

(x) Through performance, to demonstrate methods or techniques of dramatic production, or different interpretations of dramatic works.

(xi) To demonstrate decision-making processes.

(xii) by filming or observing the decision-making process, as it occurs.

(xiii) by dramatizing. and

(xiv) by simulation or role-playing.

(xv) To condense or synthesize into a coherent whole a wide range of information which, in print, would take up considerable space and would not provide the richness of background material necessary for students to appreciate fully the situation.

(xvi) To demonstrate how basic principles have been applied in the real world, where visualization of the application in its total environment is necessary to understand the way the principle has been applied, and the difficulties encountered.

(xvii) To test students'ability, by requiring them to apply concepts or principles learned elsewhere in the course; by explaining or analyzing real-life situations presented through television.

(xviii) To demonstrate the use of tools or equipment, or the efforts of tools or equipment.

(xix) To demonstrate methods of playing instruments, and the relationship between music, musicians and their instruments.í:

(xx) To increase students' sense of belonging; identification of and with course designers; to make the teaching less impersonal.

(xxi) To reduce the time required by students to master content.

(xxii) To pace students; to keep them working regularly; to break the inertia in beginning evening study.

(xxiii) To recruit or attract new students (either to the University or to specific courses); to interest general viewers in subject matters.

(xxiv) To establish academic credibility of the course to outside world.

Video-Audio Cassettes

Video Cassettes are a comparatively recent educational media. It is a child of broadcast television. The features of video cassettes and broadcast television are same. Unlike television, video cassettes can be played independent of pre-determined transmission times. The main educational advantages of television programmes are involvement, dramatic impact, dynamic properties and rich symbol content. These advantages apply equally to cassette recordings of broadcast television programmes or to video cassettes made into abinitio for using as cassettes. Video cassettes provide students full control of the medium over television broadcast. The student can watch the programme, whenever he wants and as often as he likes.

In recent years the British Open University provided a video cassette loan service for students of select courses in response to deterioration in the transmission in times available for Open University television broadcasts.

Students gave thee main reasons for borrowing cassettes:

(1) access, (2) control, and (3) level. They took advantage of the flexibility of cassettes to study the programmes at times convenient to them and in phase with

their own study patterns. They could view the programmes as often as they liked. They were able to adjust to pace of the programmes to suit their own needs, as necessary.

In the British Open University, the greatest media development in the recent times has been the audio cassettes. The University is now making more material for use on cassettes than on radio. Audio cassettes are becoming very popular. Academics like them as they can exercise control over their use and can integrate them more tightly into course design. The use of the channels-sound and vision-in acontrolled and integrated way, through the combined use of cassette and print or media, is a very powerful teaching medium. They are ranked as the most useful component next to correspondence texts. In some courses, they have been ranked as the most useful component of the course. They are liked by students because of their convenience and informality. Students frequently feel that cassettes are as good as having as personal tutorials with the course author in their rooms. Audio cassettes allow for mastery learning, explanation and discussion of graphical, tabular and printed conceptual material, practice in problem solving and exercise in mathematical processes.

Telephones

Telephone is a potential powerful educational tool. Recent years have seen a rapid growth in the use of telephone as an educational media. Teaching by telephone has been used in a number of distance education contexts and in a variety of ways with individuals and with small and large groups.

Telephone offers two way interactive communication across distance. The means of providing telephone link may be terrestial wire or cable, high frequency radio-waves, micro-waves or satellite. Although most familiar in its domestic form, telephone also has other capabilities. By means of a telephone network, audio, video and data information can be sent and received by individuals or large groups of people.

Teaching by telephone covers a variety of usage. They refer to:

- courses and students taught wholly or largely by means of an instructional telephone conferencing network with minimal accompanying printed material;
- courses taught on campus but 'attended' by distant students via a telephone link;
- courses taught partly by correspondence materials, partly by group teleconferences;
- courses taught mainly through correspondence material (perhaps with other media as well, such as television, radio oraudio cassette) and which offer supplementary tutorial support by means of telephone (either individual or group);
- courses where telephone communication is an integral part of the teaching event, for example, a live television or one-way video presentation

followed by students telephoned questions, which are both asked and answered on air;

- individual telephone calls (occasional or regular) to course writers or tutors from remote students with particular problems in understanding printed course materials;
- individual telephone calls to tutors from remote students needing advice or counselling in relation to educational problems.

In a British Open University study, telephone tutorials are found to be used effectively for the following tasks:

- to clarify student difficulties in course materials.
- to promote student discussion of specific issues and topics.
- to exchange interpretations of a case or thesis.
- to discuss problems of recent written assignments, or strategies for tackling forthcoming ones.
- to check through worked answers to previously-circulated problems.
- to analyse a written text or a musical score.
- to present short case-studies.
- to debate a prepared case for or against a thesis.
- to role-play an exercise.
- to practice and evaluate sight singing on a music course.
- to identify and clarify concept in genetics using previously circulated worksheets.
- to manipulate symbolic expressions, using previously circulated diagrammatic material.
- to construct and evaluate graphs, using previously circulated worksheets.
- to interpret and discuss previously circulated sets of raw data.
- to negotiate the design of a project in cognitive psychology and: monitor its progress.

Computers

Computers have been used extensively in education for more than twenty years, yet they have had little impact on distance education. Ehin wrote about this more than ten years ago and remarked on the absence of literature dealing specifically with computer applications in correspondence education. However, recent advances have led to increased capabilities at substantially lower costs. Two developments can be identified as most important. The first is the development and mass distribution of microcomputers; the second is the marriage of computers with communications technology, making direct and inexpensive computer communication both possible and relatively inexpensive. Computers can be used in distance education systems in two modes, referred to as local mode and transmitted mode. Local mode is synonymous with 'off line' since the computer stands alone as an independent system. Peripheral devices, such as disc drives or printers are often used to enhance the system. In transmitted mode, a computer or terminal is connected to another computer 'on line' and the operation depends upon communication between these devices. By the inter-connection of computers, it is relatively simple to create a complex learning network which could theoretically link all distance learners with their teachers and with a central institution. An electronic university could be created as described by Turnoff and established by a private enterprise firm in San Francisco. Other examples include word processing to aid course development, and data processing to aid administration and student registration.

The instructional process in distance education is divided clearly into two stages. The first stage involves the design, development, physical production and storage of instructional materials. Cooper and Thompson have discussed text processing as a powerful tool for authors and editors. Its use in creating and editing documents facilitates the development of manuscripts before the production stage. Editorial changes, additions and deletions no longer delay development or add major costs. By also providing a course writer and a course designer each with microcomputer, communications software, and a modem to connect to the telephone lines, the development process can be even more significantly enhanced. With this addition, all of the text processing options are still available, but electronic mail can be used to communicate changes and exchange materials. If a course team approach is used with multiple writers and other professionals, this approach can be extended by using computer conferencing. By adding computerised page-composing, computer graphics, and computerised photo-typesetting, the production process could also be automated, where the manuscripts (with inserted graphics) could simply be left on a data base for electronic access by learners. At present time, text processing is used by most institutions dedicated to distance teaching or having major distance education departments. Some institutions, such as the Open Learning Institute and Athabasca University also use computerised photo-typesetting systems. The course material is stored in a warehouse using a computerised inventory control system to maintain and route material.

The second stage of the instructional process involves delivery of the material to learners. Significant contributions to this area will begin to occur, when distance learners have their own personal computers (or computer terminals), although limited benefits are possible, if access to centre is provided.

Although text processing is a useful tool for student use in their assignments, the real breakthroughs here will occur through the use of computers to provide direct instruction. Computer-aided learning (CAL) has already been used at the Open University in Britain to provide diagnostic feedback, remedial help and revision aids.

It appears that many courses would benefit from the use of CAL modules. The ability of a computer to simulate real-life situations which are not available to learners due to high cost, danger of other factors, is a resource which should be brought to the distance learner. Examples are courses requiring laboratory work (such as chemistry), practical work (such as process control), decision-making (such as business or economics). Baath and Phillips and Young presented evidence to show that the use of CAL increased completion rates in distance education courses. Many learners have or can be provided with access to suitable microcomputers for at least limited periods. This would permit the inclusion of shorter CAL modules where appropriate.

Another area which promises to increase the efficiency and effectiveness of distance education is computer-managed learning. TV Ontario has already begun to make use of this method to a limited extent. In the continuing education courses, learners throughout Ontario return their assignments on computer marked sheets. The computer-managed learning software marks the assignments and automatically generates personalized letters with results and appropriate feedback. These letters are then mailed to the students using the mailing labels also generated by the computer.

The major innovation in this whole area is computerized communications. This includes electronic mail and computerized conferencing, which permit one-to-one and one-to-many communications among many people using computers and communication lines. An additional powerful feature is the ability to search and retrieve information from large-scale computerized data bases, opening up the possibility of remote libraries, such as already available with the abstracts on the ERIC system. Computer conferencing as understood here is the use of computers to link people together cross time and space. Cross has observed that computer teleconferencing is a system which enables two or more individuals at two or more locations to communicate. Without having to interrupt their work schedules and to pay for costly travel, these individuals can exchange information and learning aids. Through keyboards, terminals, printers and telephone lines, participants access a common computer for extremely efficient direct communication.

Herasim and Johnson have outlined several general features of computer conferencing systems. These include text editing, sophisticated searching capabilities for conference items, access to external databases, and electronic messaging. In addition, computer conferencing systems usually maintain a permanent record of proceeding during the course of a conference, thus serving as a type of electronic filing cabinet. Kaufman listed several other features of these systems, including:

- *Directory*—for identifying participants on the system and finding address, where messages are to be sent.
- *Electronic mail*—for one-to-one and one-to-many communications.
- *Conferences*—for group discussions, with a permanent transcript of the proceedings.
- *Private work spaces*—for collecting ideas and personal files.
- *Word Processing*—for composition and modification of message or documents.

- *Bulletin board*—for access to announcements of general or particular interests.
- *Newsletter or journal*—for access to articles or papers of general and particular interest.
- *Data bases*—for access to data or information on a variety of topics.

The final area where the computer has been extremely useful and will continue to be so, may be termed 'instructional support'. For example, the Open Learning University has been using computers in most of its internal operations. Examples include a computerized student registration system, tutor records, course development, an inventory system in the warehouse, library research database, and internal communications.

Criteria for the Use of Technology

Bates who has rich and varied experience in the use of technology in distance education and who has written extensively on the role of technology in open and distance learning suggested that distance teaching institutions decision-making on the use of technology should depend on the analysis of the following seven criteria:

- *Access*: How accessible is a particular technology for learners?How flexible is it for a particular target group ?
- *Costs:* What is the cost structure of each technology ? What is the unit cost per learner?
- *Teaching and Learning:* What kinds of learning are needed? What instructional approaches will best meet these needs? What are the best technologies for supporting this teaching and learning?
- *Interactivity and User-friendliness:* What kind of interaction does this technology enable? How easy is it to use?
- *Organisational Issues:* What are the organizational requirements, and the barriers to be removed, before this technology can be used successfully? What changes in organization need to be made?
- *Novelty:* How new is this technology?
- *Speed:* How quickly can courses be mounted with thistechnology?How quickly can materials be changed?

Bates suggests a model for technology selection and application which must have the following characteristics:

- It will work in a wide variety of contexts.
- It allows decisions to be taken at both a strategic or institution wide, level, and at a tactical, or instructional level.
- It gives equal attention to instructional and operational issues.
- It will identify critical differences between different technologies, thus enabling an appropriate mix of technologies to be chosen for any given context.
- It will accommodate new development in technology.

Selection of Valid Media Mix

The selection of valid media mix would depend upon two kinds of contexts, i.e. environmental and learning. As environmental context is concerned, media must be chosen in the light of four criteria such as availability, accessibility, acceptability and economics. As learningba: context is concerned, media must be appropriate to four criteria, such as course objectives, assessment demands, subject matters and instructional strategies.

Bates proposed twelve golden rules of using technology in education and training that apply whatever technologies are being used:

1. *Good teaching matters*: Clear objectives, good structuring of learning materials and relevance to learners' needs, all apply to the use of any technology for teaching. If these principles are ignored, then the teaching will fail, even if the unique features of the medium are exploited. Good teaching may overcome a poor choice in the use of technology, but technology will never save bad teaching.
2. *Good design is essential*: Proper instructional design is essential for proper courses.
3. *Each medium has its own aesthetic*: Each medium and technology has a different range of production skills necessary to export its unique features.
4. *Education technologies are flexible*: Technologies are flexibleand hence interchangeable in education and training. The absence of a particular technology does not necessarily present learning from being achieved.
5. *There is no super technology*: All technologies have their strengths and weakness. They therefore, need to be combined.
6. *Make all five media available*: Ensure that face-to-face, print, audio, video and digital multimedia is available for teaching purpose in one form or the other.
7. *Interaction is essential*: High quality interaction with learning materials, interaction between teachers and learners and interaction among learners are all essential for effective learning.
8. *Student numbers are critical*: The total number of learners to be served over the life of a course is a critical factor in technology selection.
9. *New Technologies are not necessarily better than old ones*: There is no law that says new technologies will automatically be better for teaching than old ones.
10. *Teamwork is essential*: No one can know everything there is to know about the educational use and design of every technology now available.
11. *Teachers need training to use technology effectively*: Teachers and instructors need training not only in the choice and use of technologies, but also in how people learn and how to teach with technology.

12. *Technology is not the issue.* The issue is: how and what do I want students learn. There is more than enough technology around now to allow you to teach in whatever way you choose.

Use of Technologies in Indian Open and Distance Learning

Indian distance education institutions are presently making use of the following technologies for distance teaching students support and institutional management:

- Radio broadcasts
- Audio Cassettes
- Audio conferencing
- Interactive radio phone-in-counselling
- TV broadcasts
- Video cassettes
- Video conferencing
- Computer associated management
- Computer mediated communications
- Computer conferencing
- Internet

India is one of the few developing countries that has made revolutionary strides in modernizing communication technologies. The first radio programme in India started in 1923 and educational use of radio began in 1930. The last three decades, in particular, have been very innovative, productive and imaginative with the development of TV, a new chapter has been added to the already widening circle of transmission systems. TV entered India five decades back in 1959 as a pilot project founded by the Ford Foundation. A significant landmark in the history of television in India was the one-year Satellite Instructional Television Experiment (SITE) launched in August 1975. An American satellite was extensively used to telecast messages since the operationalization of INSAT-1B in 1983, television network started getting spread. From the very beginning, television has been perceived as a potential tool for imparting education as an agent for social change.

The development, transfer and adoption of new technologies are not as simple as they appear. Various factors and forces influence the ease of using technologies in distance education. The problems involved in the use of technologies are multiple and critical in developing countries. The influencing factors can be categorized into five-political, economic, cultural, educational and technological. The level of technological infrastructure in a country greatly conditions the uses of technologies. India's level of technological infrastructure is low. Despite this, technologies are used in distance education institutions in India, particularly University-level distance education institutions, the distance teaching universities or open universities offering courses through the face-to-face mode and distance mode.

Research on the Use of Education Technology in Indian Open Universities

A few research studies were conducted on the use of technology in some open universities in India. On B.R. Ambedkar Open University's use of technology four research studies, which were awarded Doctoral degrees, focused on the multimedia based instructional system of BRAOU. The researchers found several weaknesses in the system and made several suggestions, some of which are the following:

1. Induction meetings for newly admitted students every year should be held at study centres for orienting students on the usefulness of technology for student learning.
2. Student Handbooks/Programme Guides for all courses should include advantages of print and non-print technologies to students in their learning.
3. Academic counsellors and study centre coordinators should motivate the students towards the use of non-print electronic media programmes.
4. All radio broadcasts and television broadcasts of the University should be put on cassettes/tapes/CDs/DVDS, and be made available to students at study centres.
5. Maximum number of study centres should be equipped with the gadgets and services necessary for presentation of electronic media programmes. In view of the increasing role of technology in distance education, the following equipment needed to be placed at maximum number of study centres of the University, and maintenance should be given top priority:
   - Telephone
   - Telephone with STD facility
   - Mobile phone
   - Tape recorder
   - Radio cum tape recorder a TV set
   - TV set with cable connection
   - TV With DTH
   - TV with MANA TV reception facility
   - VCP/VCP/DVD player
   - Computer with interest facility
   - Scanner
   - Audio cassettes
   - Video cassettes
   - Fax machine
   - Xerox machine
   - Overhead/LCD projector
6. One Sundays and other holiday, study centre should conduct additional sessions especially for presentation of audio and video programmes.
7. Media production facilities at the University headquarters should be augmented in terms of technical personnel and modern equipment

8. Interaction between academics, production staff and student support planners should be more and continuous.
9. Rational decision-making on media components of courses should happen.
10. Proper coordination is required between AIR, Doordarshan, MANA TV and University on the role of media.
11. Training in media planning and production for academics, production staff should be periodically organized with the help of EMPC, AIR, Doordarshan, MANA TV and such other organizations.
12. Training the trainers like academic counsellors coordinators of study centre and course writers to orient them to distance education system should be given top priority.

4
Digital Education

Digital education means digital learning. It is a type of learning that is supported by digital technology or by instructional practice that makes effective use of digital technology. Digital learning occurs across all learning areas and domains. Digital education gives win-win opportunities for all, at one side school, colleges and other institution finds the rapid rise in enrolments and added revenue because of digital education, and on other side students view this as a flexible and alternate option allowing them to study as per their convenient time and pace. Teachers and professors too find it convenient to prepare their teaching plans aided by digital technology. Teaching and learning becomes a smoother experience as it includes animations, gamification and audio-visual effects.

Over the last few years digital education in India is evolving at faster pace. It is changing the way students learn different concepts and theory in school and colleges. The traditional chalk and talk method in schools and colleges has been slowly changing with more interactive teaching methods as schools and colleges are increasingly adopting digital solutions.

Digital learning guarantee more participation from students as the current generation of students are well-versed with laptops, I-pads, and smart phones. There are different private players in the field of digital education like Educomp, Tata Class Edge, Pearson, and TeachNext who are continuously engaged and developing different interactive software to help teachers in classroom teaching.

Application Areas of Digitalization

Some of the areas where digitalization is concerned at greater rates are:

1. Digital India
    - Digital infrastructure as a utility to every citizen
    - Governance and services on demand
    - Digital empowerment of citizens
2. Digital Culture
3. Digital Camera
    - DSLR

- Point and shoot
- Bridge camera
- Camera phones

4. Digital Computer
5. Digital Economy
   - e-business infrastructure
   - e-business
   - e-commerce
6. Digital Economics
   - Customer expectations
   - Product enhancements
   - Collaborative innovations
   - Organisational leaderships
7. Digital Media
   - Entertainment
   - Technology
   - E-commerce
   - Health
   - Education
   - Marketing
   - Government
   - Sports
   - Environment
   - Television
   - Publishing
8. Digital versus film photography
9. Digital education

Technology Trends Pushing Up Digital Education

Today, India is one of the world's top destinations for education. With some of the best colleges and universities, it is renowned for its excellence and high standards. What's even more interesting is how technology has advanced rapidly to transform the way students in India consume educational content. Additionally, the penetration of internet-based smart phones is taking quality learning to students across geographies in India.

Today, little children are watching their favourite cartoons and learning pictorial rhymes on the same device. Education is being imparted to them through flexible and non-intrusive formats. As a consequence, students across all age groups are discovering the joys of learning and having fun while at it. There has been a noticeable shift in the perception of parents and teachers view digital learning too. Today, institutions are making efforts to shift the focus back on students to re-invent the way they learn right throughout their life.

India might not have readily adopted education technology but it's heartening to see how a traditional sector like education is using technology as an enabler so far. Today, some cutting-edge technologies are being used to further enhance this sector, while grabbing the attention of entrepreneurs, venture capitalists, corporates and governments.

1. Personalised and adaptive learning: Learning platforms, software and digital devices are together creating countless new ways to modify education. This way, the academic potential, strengths, weaknesses, aptitude and learning pace of every single student is catered to. Precise, mobile and reliable applications are being created to teach students, help them practice their learnings, take assignments and manage their schedules.

Schools are now providing their students with digital devices like desktop computers, laptops and tablets. These devices are aiding them in the teaching process while also helping them understand how students learn and how to enhance their learning process.

The 'one size fits all' teaching model is being supplemented by adaptive, personalized learning pedagogies. Going forward, this will be the new trend in formal learning that will enable students to be technologically skilled and equipped for modern workplaces.

2. Two-way conversations in E-Learning: In the traditional classroom seating scenario, students are unable to get the individual attention they need due to time constraints. In contrast, the one-to-one context of learning in digital mediums currently students to learn through videos and chat with an expert.

The upcoming 'Learning Management System' will continue the two-way communication model between students and experts. More importantly, it will let students track their coursework progress, identify improvement areas and offer ways to make the most of them.

Through the help of 'Big Data', experts will be able to capture student feedback within the framework of the content provided. With this alone, they'll be able to improvise and enhance their offerings in new ways to further benefit students.

3. Mobile-based learning: Over the past few years, mobile learning has picked up by the populace who have gradually assimilated it in their lives. It has offered students the flexibility to access educational content seamlessly across multiple digital devices like desktops, laptops, tablets and smart phones.

The smart phone user base in India continues to increase, in both urban and rural areas. The coming years will witness users accessing most of their educational content through internet powered smart phones in a massive way. Most educational content, including even online courses, will be optimized entirely for mobile devices.

4. Video-based learning: Video learning has always appealed to students since it closely mirrors the traditional classroom teaching style. Earlier, students watched video lectures as a form of homework and then discussed them during the next class. Over time, this habit brought about a remarkable improvement in their performance, with a noticeable improvement in grades. Video lectures allowed students to learn subject syllabi at their own pace and dedicate time spent in class towards interactions. This will continue to be a trend in the future where students will have access to rich and interactive content, that will be useful for both formal training as well as performance enhancement. The increase in video-based learning on mobile devices will eventually account for 80 per cent of all internet traffic by 2019.

5. Open educational resources: Open digital education resources have commonly been used in distance learning courses. They consist of freely accessible media for learning, teaching and research purposes. They are licensed to be revised and disseminated freely by teachers among students. This allows the latter to gain access to an extensive arrive of study material that is otherwise restricted indigenously.

Open educational resources also facilitate the creation of a flexible environment where teachers can customize educational content for individual sessions or classroom sittings. This is applicable for typical curricular subjects like mathematics, sciences and languages, as well as business and fine arts.

6. Usage of Virtual Reality (VR) and Augmented Reality (AR) for learning: Virtual Reality and Augmented Reality are already buzzwords in the technology space. Their advent in e-learning has massively impacted the efficiency with which it is offered to students and the way it assesses their performance.

VR allows students using e-learning platforms on mobile devices to directly interact with study material. This keeps their engagement levels high and motivates them to learn more and better. On the other hand, AR facilitates teachers and trainers in performing tasks, they previously haven't or cannot, in a safe environment.

Benefits of Digital Education

1. Benefits to Academic Institution

Academic institution can easily manage their activities with the help of digital education. Some of the important benefits are:

- Time and money of the institution will be saved.
- They can easily plan to conduct online exam and publish the exam results quickly.
- It makes knowledge to transfer easily and equally from teacher to each and every student with the help of effective and advanced technology based teaching tools.
- It helps in creating interest among which will help them in learning many concepts through interactive audio-visual teaching contents.
- Advantages over other schools and colleges which cannot provide such integrated feature-based learning and management system.
- Easy communication between institution and parents for student related academic activities.

2. Benefits to Students

As all the study contents will be taught in the classroom through multimedia slides, it creates interest and enthusiasm among the students. Learning will be fun for them. They are able to memorize many concepts through interactive audio-visual teaching conctents. Some other benefits to them are:

- They can easily view their daily time-table, class assignments, any events planned in school, etc. from home.
- They are able to prepare projects and presentation online.
- They can give online exam and view their results.
- They can easily collect teaching contents of missed lecture online.
- They can assess library online.

3. Benefits to Parents

In today's world, it is difficult for parents to visit the school or colleges because of their busy work schedule. Digital education helps the parents to view all the information of their ward from comfort of their home or office. Some of the other benefits are:

- The web facility, if digital education helps the parents to view their child's attendance record, progress in syllabus, time-table, etc.
- They can easily check the subject taught in school, homework given to their ward, any future assignments and projects and guide the ward accordingly to participate and practice.
- Easily view internal and semester exam schedule and results.
- They can easily pay the school fees and other activity charges.
- They can get information on various school events, notices, holidays and can track the presence of ward in the classroom outside the class.

4. Benefits to Teachers

Digital in education also creates interest among teachers. It helps them to make teaching interaction among students very effectively. Some other benefits are:

- It helps the teacher to mange their class time and teaching content effectively.
- They can easily avail the school as well as class related information through web.
- They can check daily time-table, assignments, teaching history, events and holiday list, self as well as student attendance, etc.
- It will help in explaining the difficult content easily and in effectively.

5. Benefits to Principals

Some of the important benefits to principals are:

- Easy to manage all the school/college activities.
- In case if he/she is on leave, he/she will be able to access all the school/ college information online and manage the school easily.
- He/she can view teachers' teaching progress and students' performance.
- It will help in allocation of class and subject to a teacher according to his/her interest and experience.
- He/she can assign tasks to other staff members and give remarks for their works.

Challenges of Digital Learning and Measure to Overcome Them

Digital learning has become very popular with period of time. But it imposes certain challenges which need to be overcome. Someone rightly said, "Digital learning should be more about the human touch that just machines". The following are the challenges of digital learning along with the measures to overcome those challenges:

Resistance to change: Every improvement has two sides of coin, with one leading to advancement and development and other relates to certain challenges associated with the implementation of this advancement. Unfamiliarity of employees towards technology is one of the biggest challenges of Digital Learning, which the mangers need to work with it. People commonly resist change, even if the changes are superior to what they had previously. They might not trust that a technology based learning programme will be as effective as interacting with an instructor. It's a fact that e-learning implementation can create enormous change within a company so implementers can expect to face some resistance.

To overcome this resistance certain measures can be taken:

- Refresher benefit feature of multimedia learning enables to makes the material more engaging and easier to assimilate. At the tome of refresher, such learning material will be at their fingertips when they want. This will enable to complete the learning within a span of time.
- Effective communication process. Communication is the key to incorporate an digital learning.
- Programme effectively. Communication will enable to understand and accept your digital learning programme quickly. It is important that trainees need to know what benefits digital learning offers them, and what are the objectives, among other aspects.

Learners motivation: Classroom which are run in the form of a seminar and discussion have the advantage of accountability and supervision.

One of the common challenges in digital learning is that, left to their own devices, employees may resent using their own time to do coursework, rather than enjoying the "vacation" from their everyday responsibilities afforded by an in-person seminar. Therefore, it becomes rather important and a big challenge on how can we keep our students motivated enough to complete the course and moreover, how can we make them enjoy the learning experience.

To overcome the challenge certain measure can be taken:

- *Incentives:* Accreditation of the courses and certification gives employees a tangible goal that benefits themselves as well as the employer. More broadly, any job training that can lead to career advancement or résumé building is valuable to today's employee.
- *Appealing:* One of the best methods to motivate your participants or audience is to make sure the digital learning courses you develop are visual and very appealing to the eye. Take a look at this info graphic, where you can get ideas on how to make eLearning more attractive.

Technological skills of learners: The digital learning implementation will be dependent upon the computer literacy of the employees using it. The ability of the learner's to access and interact with the course material dictates the utility he will get out of the programme. To overcome the resistance certain measures can be taken.

- *Adaptability:* This eLearning can be mitigated by scaling the complexity of the system to the needs of the course and other employees. When the content being taught is fairly basic, a simple interface can be used to impart it, the complexity can be scaled up as the course material and technological expertise of the learner demands.
- *Help when required:* When students run into problems while using the digital learning courses, technical support services should be there, like live chats, auto help buttons, emails, discussion boards. Availability of digital learning facilitators available will also make them feel they are supported in the programme.

Evaluating effectiveness: Yet another important challenge of digital learning is the task of determining whether the course is having the intended effect. In the absence of pop quizzes and report cards, how can an employer tell whether the eLearning implementation is achieving its goals?

Solution: Assessing the result is important, it is essential to know how many employees are using the digital learning programme, how long they spend on it, and how many complete the course, but above this it is more important to know the performance reflects their newly-acquired knowledge. If they display the skills and information gleaned from the digital learning programme in their work, then the digital learning implementation has been effective.

Challenges of Digital Education in India

Some of the major challenges for digital education in India are:

- *Resource and internet connectivity related challenges:* One of the main challenges for digital education in India is poor internet connectivity in rural areas and some part of urban areas. Majority of population across

India has still no access to internet and a large population in rural areas is still illiterate in the field of digital technology. More innovations required to make the digital education more interactive and robust.

- *Storage of trained teachers:* A major obstacle in the use of digital education in rural area is the lack of knowledge and skills. There is a shortage of teachers, formally trained on digital technology. In some of the academic institutions in rural areas, school teachers and college professors are not interested in using digital tools for conducting classes. They feel that a lot of information is explained to the students at one go through the digital medium and they prefer traditional teaching methods of chalk and blackboard. In rural areas, primary teachers and senior teachers are reluctant to get trained and adopt digital technologies for digital education in school because they are in view that these disruptive technologies are out to replace them permanently.
- *Language and content related challenge:* Language is one of the main barriers for the development of digital education in India, there are several different languages in different states have been spoken all across country pushing all the digital content in all these regional languages sometimes becomes difficult for the agencies.
- *Poor maintenance and upgradation of digital equipment:* In rural areas maintenance and upgradation of digital equipment is one of the major challenges. This is largely due to budgetary constrains by government. The digital education projects in rural schools are not self-sustainable. At inital stage various projects have been launched by government for the development of digital education, but later, they have not been taken due care for the maintenance of digital equipment which is affecting the digital education development in rural areas.
- *Insufficient funds:* Digital education involves effective and efficient usage of appropriate and latest hardware and software technology available in the market. In developing countries like India, digital technology implementation into education systems is a difficult task, as it requires huge funds and infrastructure. Through Digital India programme, the government has promised availability of funds for technology implementation but lack of insufficiency of finances leads to redundant and obsolete infrastructure and equipment in rural schools.

National Digital Library of India

The Union Ministry of Human Resource Development (HRD) launched National Digital Library of India (NDLI) on the occasion of National Reading Day Reading Day (observed on June 17) in New Delhi. NDLI's objective is to make digital educational resources available to all citizens of the country to empower, inspire and encourage learning.

NDLI is project of Ministry of HRD under the aegis of National Mission on Education through Information and Communication Technology (NMEICT) to develop a framework of virtual repository of learning resources with a single-window search facility.

NDLI has been developed by Indian Institute of Technology (IIT), Kharagpur. It is single window platform that collects and collates metadata from premier learning institutions in India and abroad, as well as other relevant sources. It is open to all at free of cost.

It is digital repository of 17 million-plus items containing textbooks, articles, videos, audio books, lectures, simulations, fiction and all other kinds of learning media in 200-plus languages from more than 170 institutions.

It has been designed to hold content of any language and provides learning and research interface support for leading Indian languages. It is arranged to provide support for all academic levels including researchers and life-long learners from all disciplines and in all popular form of access devices and also to differently-abled learners.

The National Digital Library of India also offers thousands of books, manuscripts and other digital educational content pertaining to various religions, including Hinduism, Islam, Christianity, Judaism and Zoroastrianism. Nearly 1.85 lakh items are uploaded to the digital library, which includes Hindu scriptures like Vedas and Upanishads. This massive repository of knowledge, created by a team of experts from the Indian Institute of Technology (IIT), Kharagpur on the direction of the HRD Ministry in 2015, makes multi-media digital educational resources available in various subject domains from more than 160 sources, including World e-book library and South Asia Archive of the South Asia Research Foundation.

It also contains question banks of at least 20 different competitive examinations, including the Joint Entrance Examination (JEE) conducted for admission to IITs, NITs and other centrally-funded technical institutes. "We are dedicating this digital library to the nation today. Until now, only students, teachers and institutions had access to the library. Now, we are making it accessible to everyone. Anybody can use it. It is absolutely free of cost," Education Minister said.

The NDL has already attracted 35 lakh users so far, most of whom are educational institutions, students, teachers and researchers registered on the NDL website. "Our target is to increase the number of users to three crores in a year. We will do it," Education Minister added.

To access the NDL, a user is required to register on its website. To enable people to access the digital library on their mobile phones and other Android-based devices, the NDL team has developed an application which can be downloaded from Google Play and other platforms.

More than 106 educational institutions, 12 secondary school examination boards, including that of Karnataka, have contributed to the creation of NDL by providing digital content fromtheir respective libraries. The University of Mysore,

Indian Institute of Science-Bangalore, several IITs, NITs, Indian National Academy of Science, New Delhi, Bombay High Court Judges Library, Council of Scientific and Industrial Research and Union Public Service Commission have also provided content.

Upcoming Trends in the Education Sector

1. Growing trend of Digital classroom/Flipped Classrooms: Technology is leading to a revolution in the way we learn. It is helping solve the problems of scale, quality of education, and learnability of the student. Teachers can now reach the full classroom through digital screens, enabling each child to get the same base content. Student engagement is higher as it combines various instructional styles. And each student gets exposure to world-class education, something that was just not available in a chalk and talk approach.

2. Video based learning picking up pace in India: Video-based learning makes education engaging, entertaining and exploring. The interactive preface of this segment ignites learning with a pedigree of learning out of leisure with creativity, fun and entertainment on cards via the wonderful Apps, podcasts, videos, interactive software, ebooks and online interactive electronic boards. Children are excited and operative with interest to manage the showcase via their intelligence, exploring the weak techno skills of teachers and assist them in public with pride and honour and recognition. Now the classes are student-friendly, student-operated and info-packed.

3. Popularity of online courses—MOOCS & Other distant learning programmes: Talking about the popularity of MOOCs in India, India is the second biggest market for MOOCs in the world, after the USA. It is, however, expected that India in the coming years will supersede the USA. Our country has the second largest population in the world after China and is the third in terms of university enrollment worldwide. Respectively, the USA and China are first and second for university enrollment at the moment but this may soon change.

MOOCs have opened the gateways for a lot of Indians in terms of being part of an educational revolution. It gives a great opportunity to avail high quality learning with the help of internet connectivity. Two foremost reasons as to why MOOCs is a good idea in India is millions of Indians live in poverty and are unable to afford or gain access to a higher education and secondly, there are more applicants than seats in the Indian Universities.

4. Game based learning is creating a buzz in the K-12 sector: Game based learning creates an environment where the learners easily relate themselves to and get involved. The world we have today is cultivating children who are more than just well aware of both the developments in their surroundings and their skills and abilities.

5
Digital Initiatives in Higher Education

Study Webs of Active Learning for Young Aspiring Minds (SWAYAM)

SWAYAM is an indigenous (Made in India) IT Massive Open Online Courses (MOOCs) Platform for providing best quality education that can be accessed by anyone, anytime and anywhere using the IT system.

The Concept of Massive Open Online Courses (MOOCs) involves online delivery of interactive learning content to large number of people simultaneously. It allows sharing of best quality education with everyone, thereby bringing in equity as far as the quality of education is concerned. There are 4 quadrants in the MOOC pedagogy by the MHRD and communicated to all concerned vide communication dated 11th March, 2016; and they were further updated in June 2017 after a National Convention held by Minster for HRD.

Apart from this, NMEICT has funded the National Programme on Technology Enabled Learning (NPTEL), which is a group of 7 IITs and IISc. NPTEL (http://nptel.ac.in) is a joint initiative of IITs and IISc funded by this Mission and provides e-learning through online Web and Video based courses in engineering, science and humanities streams and provides free online courseware. NPTEL have so far developed e-content in 23 Disciplines numbering 933 Courses. The NPTEL is expected to complete more than 990 Courses by December 2016. This content is also available on YouTube and on NPTEL Server and viewership of both has crossed 280 million. NPTEL takes the credit of world's most accessed Educational Channel.

Regulation

University Grants Commission (UGC) has vide Gazette Notification dated 19th July, 2016, notified Regulation, 2016 regarding 'Credit Framework for Online Learning Courses through SWAYAM'. Accordingly, a student studying at a recognised institute anywhere in the country and having cleared the Online Course through SWAYAM, shall be awarded Credits and the credits earned by such a student shall be transferred from the Host Institute to the Parent Institute where the student is studying. However, at present, the Credits upto 20 per cent of the total courses can only be earned in a Semester by such students through online learning delivered on SWAYAM platform.

Nearly 10 lakh students would be able to access courses on this Platform simultaneously. The students will be able not only to access the best teaching resources, but would also be able to interact with the teachers from anywhere in the Country using the IT systems. Backward rural areas can access teaching from the best institutes in the country electronically, thereby, raising the overall standards of higher education in the country.

SWAYAM Prabha: The 32 Educational DTH Channels

The SWAYAM Prabha has been conceived as the project for telecasting high quality educational programmes through 32 DTH channels on 24 × 7 basis. Every day, there will be new content of at least 4 hours which would be repeated 6 times a day, allowing the student to choose the time of his convenience.

DTH Channels Cover

Curriculum based course contents covering diverse disciplines, such as arts, science, commerce, performing arts, social sciences and humanities subjects, engineering, technology, law, medicine, agriculture, etc.

School education (9-12 levels) modules; for teacher training as well as teaching and learning aids to children of India to help them understand the subjects better and also help them in better preparedness for competitive examinations for admissions to professional degree programmes.

Curricula and courses that can meet the needs of life-long learners or Indian citizens in India and abroad.

IIT-PAL-to assist the students in the Classes 11 and 12 aspiring to join IITs by encouraging scientific thinking and conceptual understanding critical to answer the 'tough' questions of JEE advanced, so that good quality students enter the portals of IITs. The four channels under this would be on Mathematics, Physics, Chemistry and Biology.

The project was conceived and completed within 3 months with the active participation of the Bhaskaracharya Satellite Application Centre and Geoinformatics (BISAG), Gandhinagar and ECIL, Hyderabad.

National Digital Library (NDL)

A Project titled "Development of National Digital Library of India, Towards Building a National Asset" has been sanctioned to IIT, Kharagpur under NMEICT by MHRD. National Digital Library in India aims to collect, preserve and disseminate entire intellectual output of our country and provide online access from school level to postgraduate level, including technical education. The project aims to develop: (i) overall framework to collate large number of e-contents for school, college and higher education, e-content, virtual library, covering needs of learners with differing abilities, (ii) design & development of "OAI-PMH" Server for Metadata Harvesting, Indexed, etc., (iii) serve as a pan-India virtual teaching-learning-evaluation-knowledge platform and for key national asset, and (iv) collect resources from other Ministries such as Ministry of Culture, Health, Rural Development & Department of Science & Technology on this portal.

There are more than 72 lakh digital books available through the NDL. The contents cover almost all major domains of education and all major levels of learners from school level to the highest level of education including life-long learners. More than 15 lakh students have registered themselves in the NDL. The NDL is available through a mobile app too.

National Academic Depository

National Academic Depository is an initiative of Ministry of Human Resources Development, Govt. of India (MHRD) to facilitate digital issuance, storage, access and verification of Academic Awards issued by Academic Institutions. NAD is a Unique, Innovative and Progressive initiative under "Digital India" theme towards achieving Digital enablement of the Education Records.

NAD aspires to make the vision of Digital Academic Certificates for every Indian a reality. This touches the lives of Indian youth and empowers them with Digital, Online, Trusted, Verifiable Certificates which are accessible in a secure manner at all times. NAD promises to do away with difficulties/inefficiencies of collecting, maintaining, and presenting physical paper certificates.

e-Shodh Sindhu

More than 15,000 international electronic journals and e-books are made available to all the higher educational institutions through the e-Shodh Sindhu initiative. This allows access to be best education resources in the world using digital mode. The INFLIBNET, Gandhinagar, Gujarat is implementing the Scheme.

Virtual Labs

Physical distances and the lack of resources make us unable to perform experiments, especially when they involve sophisticated instruments. Also, good teachers are always a scarce resource. Web-based and video-based courses address the issue of teaching to some extent. Conducting joint experiments by two participating institutions and also sharing costly resources has always been a challenge. With the present day internet and computer technologies the above limitations can no more hamper students and researchers in enhancing their skills and knowledge. Also, in a country, such as ours, costly instruments and equipment need to be shared with fellow researchers to the extent possible. Web enabled experiments can be designed for remote operation and viewing so as to enthuse the curiosity and innovation into students. This would help in learning basic and advanced concepts through remote experimentation. Today, most equipment have computer interface for control and data storage. It is possible to design good experiments around some of these equipment, which would enhance the learning of a student.

Internet-based experimentation further permits use of resources—knowledge, software, and data available on the web, apart from encouraging skillful experiments being simultaneously performed at points separated in space (and possibly, time):

Virtual Lab does not require any additional infrastructural setup for conducting experiments at user premises. One computer terminal with broadband Internet connectivity in all that is needed to perform the experiments remotely.

Over 205 virtual labs in 9 Engineering & Science disciplines, comprising about 1515 experiments are operational and currently being accessed by more than 6 lakh students.

e-Yantra

An MHRD initiative under NMEICT Programme, named "e-Yantra" is implemented to incorporate Robotics into engineering education with the objective of engaging students through exciting hands-on application of mathematics, computer science, and engineering principles. Creation of robotic platforms has been very successfully demonstrated during phase-I of the project. Presently, e-Yantra has been implemented in 100 colleges. e-Yantra is creating skills by setting up lab infrastructure for project based learning and training teachers in these 100 engineering colleges. Going ahead, MHRD sees the core skills developed by IITB as generating, distributing and analyzing content to further create manpower with practical skills. All the projects and code are available on the e-Yantra website www.eyantra.org as open source content.

Campus Connectivity

Establishment of 1 GBPS Connectivity to universities and 20 512 Kbps broadband connectivity to colleges has been provisioned under NMEICT. A total of 600 Universities have been connected through 1 Gbps Optical Fibre; 22026 Colleges have so far been connected with 10 Mbps bandwidth. On the lines of 'Digital India' initiative of the PMO, the MHRD has now decided that the campuses of Universities, (having 1 Gbps bandwidth) shall be made WiFi enabled campus.

Already all the IITs, IIMs, and NITs have established WiFi campuses. The process of laying the optical fibre and provision of the WiFi in Central Universities is currently underway.

Talk to a Teacher

Talk to a Teacher developed by IIT Bombay, is an initiative of the National Mission on Education through ICT, funded by MHRD to provide free access to a few selected graduate and postgraduate courses, taught at IIT Bombay by distinguished faculty members and scholars at large. It uses A-View collaboration tool developed by Amrita University for providing virtual classrooms to the faculty across the country.

These courses can be viewed absolutely free of charge at lower bandwidths on a personal computer/laptop having a headphone and Internet connection. Registration is not required, as it does not have any evaluation/certification process. The courses are recorded live in the classrooms of IIT Bombay and may not reflect entire content of the course. Apart from the core courses in engineering and computer science disciplines, the programme also covers Humanities & Social Sciences.

More than 80,000 teachers have been trained, so far, under this project, involving synchronous delivery of courses from IIT Bombay & IIT Kharagpur.

Ask A Question: Ask A Question is a unique platform through which students from science and engineering colleges all over India can ask questions and faculty from IIT Bombay answers them. Students can ask questions either through an online forum or during an interactive live session. Interactive live sessions are held on every Thursday from 4:00 P.M to 5:00 P.M in the field of Electrical Engineering and every Friday from 4:00 P.M to 5:00 P.M in the field of Physics.

e-Acharya

e-Acharya also called 'Integrated e-Content Portal' of NMEICT, is the official repository of NMEICT e-content and all content produced under NMEICT is being put at this Repository platform at INFILIBNET Centre Gandhinagar, so to apply basic tenets of preservation for digital content, implement standard Metadata schema of different types for the digital content and ensure their long-term availability.

All the Project Investigators awarded development of e-Content under NMEICT have been requested to ensure the deliverables are placed, at the earliest, in the Integrated Portal/e-Acharya of MHRD. Further, the NCERT shall provide e-content Links to e-Acharya and the NOIS shall provide the content on HDD to the e-Acharya repository and both shall ensure that all the content including e-Books are made available on e-Acharya. The e-Acharya besides a repository of content shall also have the Metadata of all these contents and it shall form a vertical of 'National Digital Library' (NDL), being implemented by the IIT Kharagpur.

The e-Acharya shall be backed by a robust 24X7 Data Centre, which shall be integrated with NMEICT, Cloud network, set up at NIC/NKN Data Centre by the IIT Delhi and called 'Baadal'. The MOOCs being produced under NMEICT shall also be uploaded on e-Acharya.

e-Kalpa

Another MHRD/NMEICT initiative named "e-Kalpa" creating Digital-Learning Environment for Design in India has successfully demonstrated the achievement of the following project objectives, on completion of its phase-I:

1. Digital online content for learning Design with e-Learning programmes on Design.

2. Digital Design Resource Database including the craft sector.
3. Social networking for Higher Learning with collaborative Learning Space for Design.
4. Design inputs for products of National Mission in Education through ICT as on December 2015, the content of e-Kalpa website named "D'source" includes 160 Courses on Design Learning in different domains, more than 400 Resources in the form of fine examples of Design and crafts, 110 Case studies of Design Projects undertaken by professionals and design students, 50 Video lectures and presentations by subjects experts and 600 examples of a visual Gallery that has documented works of the rich tradition of art and design seen across different regions of India.

Free and Open Source Software for Education (FOSSEE)

FOSSEE project sanctioned to IIT Bombay has been promoting use of open source software in educational institutions (http://fossee.in). It does through instructional material, such as spoken tutorials, documentation, such as textbook companions, awareness programmes, such as conferences, training workshops, and Internships.

Textbook Companion (TBC) is a collection of code for solved examples of standard textbooks. About 2,000 college students and teachers have participated in this activity & close to 1,000 TBCs have been created in Scilab and Python alone. FOSSEE has made all the TBCs open source and has made them available for free download. Scilab and Python TBCs are also on the cloud, so that one needs only a browser to access/execute the codes of TBC.

FOSSEE is promoting the well established open source software: OpenFOAM, an alternative to the proprietary software Fluent for computational fluid dynamics; DWSIM, an alternative to the proprietary software Aspen Plus, for chemical process simulation. FOSSEE has also undertaken several new open source software activities as well: raising Scilab toolboxes to that of Matlab; development of eSim, an electronic design automation software, an alternative to ORCAD; development of Sandhi, a software for data acquisition and control, an alternative to LabVIEW. The FOSSEE team works on open source hardware projects, such as Open PLC and Arduino as well. Through all of these projects, a large number of students across the country have been trained.

e-Vidwan

The 'Information and Library Network' (INFLIBNET) Centre took the initiative called "Vidwan: Expert Database and National Researcher's Network" with the financial support from NMEICT. The objectives of VIDWAN are to—

i) collect academic and research profiles of scientists, faculty and research scientists working in leading academic and R&D organizations in India and abroad;

ii) quickly and conveniently provide information about experts to peers, prospective collaborators, funding agencies, policy-makers and research scholars in the country;
iii) establish communication directly with the experts who possess the expertise needed by research scholars;
iv) identify peer reviewers for review of articles and research proposals; and
v) create information exchanges and networking opportunities among scientists.

The database can be used for selection of panels of experts for various committees and taskforces established by the Ministries/Govt. establishments for monitoring and evaluation purposes. Further, the availability of single point expert database will help the policy-makers and funding agencies in decision-making and policy intervention. As on 31st December, 2015, the database contains more than 17,500 profiles of experts from 2,000 leading academic institutions, universities, R&D organizations including IITs, CSIR, DRDO, etc.

Central Cloud Infrastructure

The MHRD under NMEICT has awarded a project to IIT Delhi, to set up a robust 24X7 backed Data Centre and the activities have been put up at NIC/NKN Data Centre, and the cloud is called 'Baadal'. The IIT Delhi cloud is hosting e-content and video content of e-Acharya.

6
Computer Education

In this era of science and technology, computer education has become an integral part of every profession. Computer programmes these days are dominating almost every domain of our life. We have entered a virtual world and have become so used to it that now stepping back is not possible. Everyone has to build their capacities on the computer as the virtual utility device and explore the skills in their own field of specialization; to Pexplore and demonstrate the professional capacities. To build in such professional specialization by building programmes, short and long-term courses, vocational education programmes, etc. have designed with a rigorous combination of practical relevancies that the students can prove their selves and contribute in reality. It would not be wrong to say that the computers, as well as the computer generated softwares are accelerating the developmental process of the developed as well as developing countries. Computers have been long used to perform some data generation as well as formulation, simulation, communication, for instructional games and education, etc. but during past few years the use of computer technology saw a great boost, which can be attributed to the constant development in the field of science and technology as well as new innovations that have made technology really affordable even for the common masses.

The computer education or the prevailing IT revolution in the country can help the current economy as well as the education system in the following ways:

- In the field of education by providing various user-friendly programmes have an interactive interface and that children do like while they study. This can boost the interest of the student as well as teacher and the result is some effective learning outputs.
- Improving the performance of various government schemes aimed to reach common people. Putting computer as well as IT in use over here, assessing the reach of the scheme can be easily accessed using various user interface programmes. Also, computer programmes are capable of providing information about a particular beneficiary as well are within a few seconds, just with a click of the mouse.

- Computer programmes provide reliable, an effective administration that too at an affordable price. With computer being put to use in various administrative departments the workload on employees have reduced considerably. Large heaps of files lying in government department have been converted into a small space on the CPU of the system. Also, this has led to the increases in the efficiency of the administrative offices and grievances, if any can be handled very quickly and there is no need to look in for the file from the huge heaps of files.
- Trained IT officials from India are securing jobs in some reputed institutions as well as in big organization across the world, thus making the country proud.
- Computer-based simulation programmes can effectively be used training purpose.

Computers in Education

Computers have changed the way we work, be it any profession. Therefore, it is only natural that the role of computers in education has been given a lot of importance in recent years. Computers play a vital role in every field. They aid industrial processes, they find application in medicine; they are the reason why software industries developed and flourished and they play an important role in education. This is also why the education system has made computer education a part of school curriculum. Considering the use of computer technology ixn almost every sphere of life, it is important for everyone to have at least the basic knowledge of using computers. Let's look at what role computer technology plays in the education sector.

Computer technology has had a deep impact on the education sector. Thanks to computers, imparting education has become easier and much more interesting than before. Owing to memory capacities of computers, large chunks of data can be stored in them. They enable quick processing of data with very less or no chances of errors in processing. Networked computers aid quick communication and enable web access. Storing documents on computers in the form of soft copies instead of hard ones, helps save paper. The advantages of computers in education primarily include:

1. Storage of information
2. Quick data processing
3. Audio-visual aids in teaching
4. Better presentation of information
5. Access to the Internet
6. Quick communication between students, teachers and parents

Computer teaching plays a key role in the modern education system. Students find it easier to refer to the Internet than searching for information in fat books. The process of learning has gone beyond learning from prescribed textbooks.

Internet is a much larger and easier-to-access storehouse of information. When it comes to storing retrieved information, it is easier done on computers than maintaining hand-written notes.

1. Computers are a brilliant aid in teaching: Online education has revolutionized the education industry. Computer technology has made the dream of distance learning, a reality. Education is no longer limited to classrooms. It has reached far and wide, thanks to computers. Physically distant locations have come closer due to Internet accessibility. So, even if students and teachers are not in the same premises, they can very well communicate with one another. There are many online educational courses, whereby students are not required to attend classes or be physically present for lectures. They can learn from the comfort of their homes and adjust timings as per their convenience.

2. Computers have given impetus to distance education: Computers facilitate effective presentation of information. Presentation software like PowerPoint and animation software like Flash among others can be of great help to teachers while delivering lectures. Computers facilitate audio-visual representation of information, thus making the process of learning interactive and interesting. Computer-aided teaching adds a fun element to education. Teachers hardly use chalk and board today. They bring presentations on a flash drive, plug it into a computer in the classroom, and the teaching begins. There's colour, there's sound, there's movement-the same old information comes forth in a different way and learning becomes fun. The otherwise not-so-interesting lessons become interesting due to audio-visual effects. Due to the visual aid, difficult subjects can be explained in better ways. Things become easier to follow, thanks to the use of computers in education.

3. Computer software help better presentation of information: Internet can play an important role in education. As it is an enormous information base, it can be harnessed for retrieval of information on a variety of subjects. The Internet can be used to refer to information on different subjects. Both teachers and students benefit from the Internet. Teachers can refer to it for additional information and references on the topics to be taught. Students can refer to web sources for additional information on subjects of their interest. The Internet helps teachers set test papers, frame questions for home assignments and decide project topics. And not just academics, teachers can use web sources for ideas on sports competitions, extraT: curricular activities, picnics, parties and more.

4. Computers enable access to the Internet which has information on literally everything: Computers enable storage of data in the electronic format, thereby saving paper. Memory capacities of computer storage devices are in gigabytes. This enables them to store huge chunks of data. Moreover, these devices are compact. They occupy very less space, yet store large amounts of data. Both teachers and students benefit from the use of computer technology. Presentations, notes and test papers can be stored and transferred easily over computer storage devices. Similarly, students can submit homework and assignments as soft copies. The process becomes paperless, thus saving paper. Plus, the electronic format makes data storage more durable. Electronically erasable memory devices can be used repeatedly. They offer robust storage of data and reliable data retrieval.

5. *Computer, hard drives and storage devices are an excellent way to store data:* This was about the role of computers in education. But we know, it's not just the education sector which computers have impacted. They are of great use in every field. Today, a life without computers is unimaginable. This underlines the importance of computer education. Knowledge of computers can propel one's career in the right direction. Computers are a part of almost every industry today. They are no longer limited in any specific field. They are used in networking, for information access and data storage and also in the processing and presentation of information. Computers should be introduced early in education. I don't think I am making an overstatement in saying that computer education is as fundamental as learning English. Yes, it is.

Ways in which Computers Assist in Teaching and Learning

1. *To replace writing on the chalkboard/while board/overhead:* Instead of writing on the board, instructor or a student takes notes on the computer and projects this onto the screen so that whole class can see this. Purposes:

- Enables the students to read what has been written more easily than instructor's handwriting.
- This can then be saved as a record of class (summary of class discussion or group work), then e-mailed to the whole class or posted on the course with page.
- Students can work in small groups and use laptop computers to take notes on their group's discussions (replacing the use of poster paper or handwriting over head transparencies). When they share their group's findings with the whole class, they copy their work to disk and bring it up to the front of the class to project using the instructor's computer.

2. *PowerPoint-to replace slides, pre-prepared overhead transparencies, and even video:*

- Creating own presentations for class.
- Creating own presentations for class and uploading these to course web page.
- Using presentations that come on CD with textbook.
- Having students create PowerPoint presentations to give presentations in class and for presenting assignments.
- Creating presentations but printing them out and creating overhead transparencies of the slides (where faculty members does not have access to a computer in the classroom or does not feel comfortable with giving PowerPoint presentations.

3. Course Web Pages: (Either using TopClass course assignment system or faculty member creating own site using PageMill or other web-authoring software).

- Having a collection of pages for each course (a course site) that includes some or all of the following: syllabus, class schedule, assignments, links to readings, on-line class discussion, posting of student work, on-line testing.

4. Internet: Outside of class:

- Required readings (having students read specific web pages as assignments). Especially useful: online journals (e.g. ISTE)
- Student research (for sites on specific topics)

In-class use:

- Instructor integrating websites into teaching of lesson (projecting sites on the screen)
- Having students use specific sites during class, other working in groups, using their laptops, or in computer lab, with one or two students per computer.
- Having students integrate websites into class presentations (so that as students presents to the class, they project the website onto the screen and use this as part of their presentations).

5. Online Discussion Forums: Using TopClass, Web Crossing or Tom Bacig's board.

- Students so continue class discussions outside of class
- Outside speakers can join in class discussions online
- Using folders within the discussion forum, students can "meet" online to do group projects
- Distance education classes can meet on net.

6. Student Created Web Pages:

- Students creating on-line portfolios of their work
- Class developed "clearing house" on particular tasks or topics
- As a means of students sharing their work with peers (for group assignments) or with the instructor

7. Class E-mail Alias:

- For instructor to provide updates and reminders to students
- To e-mail students copies of work developed in class (e.g. instead of writing on the board, instructor or a student takes notes summarizing class discussion or group work, and then this is e-mailed to the whole class).

Obstacles in Using Computers

1. Classroom Set-up

- Room arrangement size makes it difficult to bring in a computer cart or for all students to be able to see the screen
- Lighting:
  - Too light so screen can't be seen (no blinds curtains)
  - Can only turn all lights o or all off. All on is too bring, and all off is too dark (students can't see instructor, each other, and or their notes)
- No Ethernet connections for students, so they cannot access the internet during class for purposes of group or individual work

2. Equipment

- InFocus projector controls locked in cabinet and instructor doesn't have key, too time consuming to have to get the key before every class.
- No permanent InFocus projector in class, so instructor has t check one out each time.
- No time to pick up check-out computer carts before class (especially for instructors with little time between classes).
- InFocus projectors on cats are not always ready to use (enables are not attached or may be missing)
- Because of variety of InFocus projectors, instructors may not be familiar with using all of them and thus, have difficult configuring their laptop to work with the projector.
- Resolution of Mac Computers with most of the InFocus projectors is not very clear,
- Takes too long to set up the equipment, if instructor has to bring own laptop and connect it. This is an issue for instructors who have back-to-back classes in different rooms or who have to wait for another class to leave the room before they can go in and set up for their class.

3. Internet issues

- Connection to internet may be slow or unreliable. Instructors need to be able to make connections to access course site, outside sites, an UMD server.
- Quality of websites: Students are still not discerning consumers and are not differentiating between reputable and poor sites.
- Students' over reliance on the internet for research (many not using the library at all).
- Students are plagiarizing work from the internet.

4. Accessibility and equity issues

- Not all students have access to the internet off campus (and even on campus) and are thus, being disadvantaged by classes they place heavy emphasis on use of the internet.

- For some commuters from outside of the region in rural areas dialing UMD on their internet service provider is a long distance call and thus becomes very costly.
- Not all students are comfortable using computers (in and out of class).

5. Instructor use

- Creating computer based materials for class is very time consuming, especially for begninng users.
- Learning the necessary skills up-to-date is very time consuming.
- Even once an instructor has a course website online, mandating it is time consuming (especially checking to see that external links are working and monitoring online class discussions).
- Over reliance or inappropriate use of computers as a teaching tool can compromise teaching and learning effectiveness.

6. Academic snobbery

- Colleagues perceive its use as attempts to be "showy" or spoon feeding.

Real Life Uses of Computers in Education

Teaching-Learning process

Instructions:

- Instructing the students using PowerPoint slides, Word documents or Web pages and using hyperlinks for better concept clarity.
- Helps in improving pronunciation of students by using microphones, headphones, speakers, specially prepared software and special dedicated websites.
- Video conferencing, chat and email helps in better communication, hence better concept clarity. Also concept of e-tutor has given access to teachers instantly and given teachers a better chance to earn.
- Current syllabus can be viewed through website of the concerned school board; made available to students, if teacher has made a website and uploaded using Internet; and updating-using web could be done easily.
- Inspiring students to express their imagination using Paint Brush
- Encouraging the students to surf web pages and gather relevant detailed information through web pages.
- Readymade software could give practice material to students.

Learning:

- Collecting notes/pictures/videos from web pages for detailed information and projects/assignments.
- Saving the documents as soft copy for future use
- Learning through animations, as they are much near to the students

- e-books/online libraries/online encyclopedias help to guide in minutes and save precious time and resources.
- Creating videos using images, albums for better power point slides.
- Simulated Learning gives them an idea of the real situation.
- Publication of pamphlet/brochures for awareness with institution and among community members.

2. Testing and Evaluation process

- Keeping records of students for their academic scores
- Keeping records in relation to personal history
- Creating question bank for students
- Using computers for testing by asking questions from question bank
- Online Testing and Evaluation
- Analysis and interpretation of the data
- Previous year Question papers and sample papers using websites.

3. Guidance purposes

- With reference to collective records of the students maintained year-wise, stored in computers
- Testing for aptitude, interest, psychology using computer data bases and internet.

4. Library

- Documents stored as soft copy for students/faculty members use
- Online magazines, journals, brochures, research articles
- Records of the books/record of the books maintained using special library software.
- Records of the issues and returns of the books.

5. School Administration

- Records of students (personal, academic, financial)
- Records of employees of school
- Accounts of the institution
- Decision making process
- Aid to memory with minimum paper work
- Eye on current regulations of government and affiliating school boards and related authorities
- School canteen for billing
- Fees collection and maintenance of fees record.
- Circulation of instruction/notices and getting it in printed form
- Preparation of school magazine.

Framework for using Computers in Education

- Computers in the modern society

- Basic computer hardware
- Software application packages (like word processors, spreadsheets, multi-media, etc.) and their utility in education
- Development of Question Bank and interactive quizzes for evaluation
- Using Internet as communicative and research tool
- e-learning
- Copyright issues and the relative issues
- Computer Assisted Instructions
- Computers Enhancing Teaching Learning Process
- Integration of Technology with Education
- Lesson plans demonstrating use of computers in teaching

Apart from theoretical paper, there must be a practical compulsory examination based on the framework which should be of more weightage. Focus should be made on demonstrating use of computers in Teaching-Learning process. Practical must include demonstration of e-learning process; especially web conference, preparation of slides, and creation of result with analysis of same and so on.

A suggestive syllabus based on the above framework is given so as to at least, view a directive sample.

Computers in Education (Core Paper)

A MODEL SYLLABUS

Objectives:

After completing the prescribed syllabus, the students will be able to:

- Appreciate the use of computers in enhancing Teaching-Learning Process
- Identify the main components of the hardware in use (i.e. Central Processing Unit (CPU), input devices, output devices and storage devices)
- Use software application packages skillfully and intelligently for producing structured educational material for use in several subjects which are their core and methodology papers.
- Demonstrate an understanding of how one can communicate with a computer online for sources of information, as well as with other people using a network.
- Browse the internet and conduct research for their lessons
- Evaluate digital lessons plans, project, presentations and research
- Appreciate the concept of integration of technology with education

Contents

Unit I: Introduction to Computers

- Place of computers in our society
- Computers—Meaning and characteristics
- Classification of computers (based on size and purpose)
- Hardware Components
  - Input Devices (Keyboard, Mouse, Scanner, Microphone, Joystick, Web Camera, Digital Camera)
  - Processing Devices (CPU and its components)

- ➢ Memory Devices (Primary-RAM, ROM; Secondary-Hard Disk, Floppy Disk, CD-ROM, Pen Drive)
- ➢ Output Devices (Monitor, Printer, Speakers, LCD Projectors)

- Software Components (System software, Application software)
- Computer Networks (LAN, MAN, WAN)
- Introduction to Basic Computer Screen [Operating System, start/shutting of the computer, Exploring Desktop Icons, Managing folders, Basic Commands (cut, copy, paste, saving/accessing a file].
- Using 'Paint' as a drawing tool
- Scan and Print document/picture
- Computer care and computer lab maintenance.
- Computers Enhancing Teaching-Learning Process.

Unit II: Software Application Packages and Question Bank Development

- Word Processors
  - ➢ Apart from basic options of a Word processor; focus on: Creating and saving a new document, drawing tables, hyperlinks, mail merge and macro.
  - ➢ Word Processors enhancing Teaching Learning Process
- Spreadsheets
  - ➢ Apart from basic options of a spreadsheet; focus on: Data inserting, sorting and analyzing, using formulae, presenting data on charts.
  - ➢ Spreadsheets enhancing Teaching Learning Process
- Multi-media presentations
  - ➢ Apart from basic options of Power Point; focus on: Storyboarding of presentations (emphasis on content), adding images, videos, animations, transitions and hyperlinks to the slides.
  - ➢ Multimedia enhancing Teaching Learning Process
- Question Bank Development
  - ➢ Developing Question Bank using Hot Potatoes with different types of questions such as multiple choice, short answers, jumbled sentences, crossword, match, order, gap-fill exercises.
  - ➢ Hot Potatoes enhancing Teaching-Learning Process

Unit III: Internet

- **Basics of Internet**
  - ➢ Define terms related to the Internet
  - ➢ Enter an address to locate a specific Web site
  - ➢ Explore various sites on the World Wide Web
  - ➢ Use hyperlinks in Web pages
  - ➢ View educational resources on the World Wide Web
- **Search engines as research tool**
  - ➢ Use a search engine to locate information on the World Wide Web
  - ➢ Describe good search techniques
- Internet as communication tool for peer interaction/expert consultation
  - ➢ Create and send electronic mail

- ➢ Read messages posted on an Internet discussion group/board
- ➢ Use an education-related chat room on the Internet
- ➢ Conduct video-conferencing
- ➢ Blogs to encourage interaction
- ➢ Role of internet in collaborative projects
- Examine and critically evaluate a Website
  - ➢ Computer virus
  - ➢ Ensuring students safety on the internet
  - ➢ International copyright issues regarding computer technology and internet

Unit IV: Integrating Technology with Education

- Computer Assisted Instructions (Meaning), Difference between Computer Assisted Instructions and Conventional Teaching.
- Using technology to promote higher order thinking skills and develop curriculum framing questions.
- Technology supported project based learning
- Development of projects depicting integration of technology with education projects.

Computer Courses in India

Degree Courses in Computer

- BCA (Hardware & Networking)
- Bachelor of Computer Applications in Hardware and Networking
- BCA (Mobile Applications Development)
- Bachelor of Computer Applications in Mobile Applications Development
- MSc (Hardware & Networking)
- Master of Science in Hardware & Networking

Diploma Courses in Computer

- Advance Diploma in Computer Science & Engineering
- Diploma in Computer Multimedia
- Diploma in Computer Science
- Diploma in Hardware Maintenance
- Post Graduate Diploma in Advanced Computing (PG-DAC)
- Post Graduate Diploma in Front Office
- Post Graduate Diploma in Hardware Maintenance and Networking (PGDHMN)

Certificate Courses in Computer

- Basic Computer Course (BCC)
- Agriculture Science and Technology Courses
- Architecture Courses
- Arts Courses
- Civil Aviation Courses

- Commerce Courses
- Engineering Courses
- Fashion Interior Designing Courses
- Hospitality and Tourism Courses
- Information Technology Courses
- Jewelry Designing Courses
- Law Courses
- Mangment Courses
- Maritime and Naval Courses
- Mass Communications Courses
- Medical Courses
- Multimedia Animation and Gaming Courses
- Professional Courses
- Radio TV and Film Production Courses
- Science Courses
- Yoga and Naturopathy Courses

National Institute of Computer Education (NICE)

The National Institute of Computer Education (NICE), mission is a unit of National Account as well as Computer Education Trust registered under the Public Charitable Trust Act 1882 under section 60 videos (Reg. No. 948/09), society registration act 21, 1860 (Reg. No S/64772) from Govt. of India NCT, New Delhi, respectively and working in computer and Accounts field with the central as well as state Govt. to reach every class of the society. The Institute is also certified by ISO 9001:2008 Certified Institute. NICE appreciated by State government and Government of India.

The NICE is a very important as well much-needed step towards the computer education in the country. Computers, as well as IT revolution, is ruling every domain of human life, whether it is the banking sector, health, education or administration, computers are being used in every field these days. In this era of Information Technology and Science, the institute is committed to making available the computer education literacy and accounts education on very nominal fee structures across the country covering the rural and urban area. Through TCRD (Training Centre for Rural Development) as well as TCGD (Training centre for Global development).

NICE is known as the pioneer of computer literacy throughout the country and is committed to providing quality education in the field of IT at a very affordable cost to both rural as well as urban students and professionals. NICE is focussed on the main objective that is to provide general environment opportunities for its student by preventing the best-designed job-oriented courses and jobs. Computer literacy to every eligible candidate of the country.

NICE provides in a large number of diploma, certificate courses as well as professional courses. Some of these are:

- Diploma in Office Accounting and publishing (DOAP)
- Diploma in Computer Application (DCA)
- Diploma in Computer Application Web Technology (DCAWT)
- Diploma in Computer Programming (DCP)
- Diploma Web Hosting (DWH)
- Professional Accounting Business System (PABS)
- Professional Course in Auto Cad (PCA)
- Professional Course in Desk Top Publishing (DTP)
- Professional Course in Tally (Tally)
- Professional Course in C Language (C)
- Professional Course in C++
- Professional Course in JAVA

Indian Computer Education Society (ICES)

Another pioneer institute in the field of computer as well as technical education is Indian Computer Education Society (ICES) that started functioning as a voluntary organization in 1990, when computer education was not widespread as in today's time, in fact, it would not be wrong to say that computer education was in its infantile stage at that time. Though the starting was not easy, still it was the strong will of few volunteers who were motivated enough to make a start despite various technical as well as cultural roadblocks. There was a lot of exploitation in the field and the commuters were only city dwellers. There were a lot of limitations at that time, technology was not commonly affordable and computer books were very dear and affordable only to the affluent. Hence, there was a major challenge to reach the common masses.

With a vision that India can prosper only if the IT education is spread far and wide, and jobless young are initiated into it, the Society was registered in the same year (K.912/90) under the Travancore-Cochin Charitable Institution Act, 1955, and thus, encouraged educated as well as not so well-qualified jobless youths to start computer centers in as many places as possible, printed and provided the centre with low-cost-study aid materials, conducted several IT shows and exhibitions across the areas and thus, introducing immense possibilities of Information Technology. This was not the only achievement, the ICES also assisted the state government as an empanelled Agency for the IT School project during 2002-07, started a campus at Kochi with all infrastructural facilities to provide them with an up-to-date training to the resource persons in member institutes and grew by leaps and bound by spreading to TamilNadu, Goa, UP and Hyderabad with well-equipped member institutes. Besides ICES computer Courses it is affiliated to Guru Jambheswar University of Science & Technology, Hisar, Monomania Sudaranar University, TamilNadu CDAC Gist Pace for all computer courses and IETE Computer Poly-Technical for SSLC passed. ICES offer five types of courses:

- Diploma Courses
- C-DAC Courses
- Certificate Courses
- IETE Courses
- University Courses

All India Computer Saksharta Mission

Yet another step towards the computer education was taken in the form of India Computer Saksharta Mission, an autonomous institution registered under Act. 21, 1860 Reg. No. S/55556 by the Government of India NCT, New Delhi and Act, 1882 Under Section 17 Vide Reg. No. 4219/IV/Delhi. Soft Aim (Mrudu Dheya) Education Foundation. Gujarat Certificate Registered. In Employment Exchange, M.P. Govt. Reg. No. 1801-1871. AICSM, RJITS & RJSS provides various training programmes of Central and State Government to the people of different categories in the society. The main aim of the AICSM is to fulfill the dream of Government of India, "Information Technology for everyone", and to fulfill the needs of more than Lakhs of IT professional in India and other jobs related to this factor and giving the employment directly or indirectly to one million people of India, "All India Computer Saksharta Mission" the main motto behind running this programme is to bring computer revolution in every village and city of India by delivering the quality technical education at the nominal fee to the people of every category in India. Different certificate courses available are:

- Certificate in Microsoft Office (CMO)
- Certificate in DTP (CD)
- Advance CAD/CAM Course (Complete CAD/CAM training for CNC lathe and CNC milling)
- 3D Designing (CAD Course)
- CNC Operating

7
Online Education

Online education is a type of educational instruction that is delivered via the internet to students using their home computers. During the last decade, online degrees and courses have become popular alternative for a wide range of non traditional students, include those who want to continue working full-time or raising families. Most of the time, online degree programmes and courses are offered via the host school's online learning platform, although some are delivered using alternative technologies. Although there are subtle dissimilarities, the main difference between online and traditional learning is the fact that online education liberates the student from the usual trappings of on-campus degree programmes—including driving to school, planning their schedule around classes, and being physically present for each sequence of their coursework.

If this sounds drastic, it really isn't. The truth is, the education methods and materials provided in online degree programmes are often the same as those provided for on-campus programmes.

Although online education is often similar to on-campus instruction, it can be delivered in a number of ways. Distance learning is usually offered using one of these methods, or a combination of them:

- *100 per cent Online Education:* Fully-online degrees are earned from the comfort of your own home with no required visits to your college or university campus.
- *Hybrid Education:* Hybrid education allows students to pursue a combination of online and on-campus courses.
- *Online Courses:* While online courses may be part of a degree programme, they can also be taken on their own in order to master a certain subject or learn a specific skill.
- *MOOCs:* MOOCs, or massive open online courses are usually delivered in lecture form to online "classrooms" with as many as 10,000 people.

No matter which type—or types—of online education one chooses to pursue, the options are typically plentiful. Where online education put down roots in just a handful of college majors, it has since expanded to nearly every field and discipline in academia, with very few exceptions.

What is Online Learning?

Online in education takes place over the Internet. It is often referred to as "e-learning" among other terms. However, online learning is just one type of "distance learning"-the umbrella term for any learning that takes place across distance and not in a traditional classroom. Distance learning has a long history and there are several types available today, including:

- *Correspondence Courses:* conducted through regular mail with little interaction.
- *Telecourses:* where content is delivered via radio or television broadcast.
- *CD-ROM Courses:* where the student interacts with static computer content.
- *Online Learning:* Internet-based courses offered synchronously and/or asynchronously.
- *Mobile Learning:* by means of devices, such as cellular phones, PDAs and digital audio players (iPods, MP3 players).

By far the most popular approach today is online education. According to the Sloan Consortium, online enrolments continue to grow at rates faster than for the broader student population and institutes of higher education expect the rate of growth to continue increasing. Some of the key findings:

- Over 1.9 million students were studying online in the fall of 2003.
- Schools expect the number of online students to grow to over 2.6 million by the fall of 2004.
- Schools expect online enrollment growth to accelerate—the expected average growth rate for online students for 2004 is 24.8 per cent, up from 19.8 per cent in 2003.
- The majority of all schools (53.6%) agree that online education is critical to their long-term strategy.
- A majority of academic leaders believe that online learning quality is already equal to or superior to face-to-face instruction. (The "no significant difference" phenomenon.)

Types of Online Courses

- Flipped courses, instructors record their lectures or use open-source resources to provide the lecture content.
- Hybrid course
- Face-to-face
- Web-based
- Web-enhanced
- Peer instruction
- MOOC

Ten Advantages to Online Education

1. Variety of programme and courses: From traditional four-year universities to completely online career colleges, higher education today offers a variety of options for students. This means that no matter what students study, from nursing to neuroscience, they can find the courses or programmes they need online. Students can also earn every academic degree online, from a career certificate to a doctorate.

2. Lower total costs: Online programmes prove a more affordable option than traditional colleges. Though not all online degrees offer less expensive net tuition prices than traditional colleges, associated expenses almost always cost less. For example, there are no commuting costs, and sometimes required course materials, such as textbooks, are available online at no cost. In addition, many colleges and universities accept credits earned via free massive open online courses (MOOCs), the most recent advance in online education. These free online courses can help students fulfill general education requirements.

3. More comfortable learning environment: Commercials that feature online students studying in their pajamas only skims the surface of one of the benefits of online education: no physical class sessions. Students listen to lectures and complete assignments sent to them electronically, with no need to fight traffic, leave work early for class, or miss important family time.

4. Convenience and flexibility: Online courses give students the opportunity to plan study time around the rest of their day, instead of the other way around. Students can study and work at their convenience. Course material is always accessible online, making special library trips unnecessary. All of these benefits help students balance work and family commitments with their education.

5. More interaction and greater ability to concentrate: While contradictory evidence about the rate of online student participation versus participation in traditional courses exists, one thing remains certain: Online courses offer shy or more reticent students the opportunity to participate in class discussions more easily than face-to-face class sessions. Some students even report better concentration in online classes due to the lack of classroom activity.

6. Career advancement: Students can take online courses and even complete entire degrees while working, while in-between jobs, or while taking time to raise a family. This academic work will explain any discontinuity or gaps in a resume as well. Also, earning a degree can show ambitiousness to prospective employers and a desire to remain informed and prepared for new challenges.

7. Continue in your profession: Even if someone wants to complete a degree, it may not mean they want to leave their current job. For most students today, increasing college costs mandate that some students continue working while in school. The previously mentioned flexibility of online programmes enable students to keep working while also pursuing academic credentials.

8. Avoid commuting: During snowstorms and thunderstorms, colleges may cancel classes to avoid putting commuting students at risk of dangerous driving conditions. Rather than miss important class sessions, students in online courses can always "attend" by participating in discussion boards or chat sessions, turning in their work on time, and watching lectures or reading materials. Many students also find substantial savings on fuel costs with no commute for classes.

9. Improve your technical skills: Even the most basic online course requires the development of new computer skills, as students learn to navigate different learning management systems (LMS) and programmes. The participation skills students learn within their online courses translate to many professions, including creating and sharing documents, incorporating audio/video materials into assignments, completing online training sessions, etc. Some schools even offer students free laptops or iPads.

10. Transfer credits: For college students who want to attend summer classes, but live too far from their colleges and/or work summer jobs, taking online classes from an accredited college and transferring the credits to their primary college can be beneficial. Students can earn college credit while still enjoying their summer vacation or fulfilling the responsibilities of their seasonal employment. Similarly, if a college or university does not offer enough open sections of a required course, students can take the course online at another college and transfer the credits.

Students in online programmes can effectively manage their time, learn the materials, and complete assignments on their own schedules to name just a few benefits of online learning.

Online Education—FAQ

Those new to online education are often unclear about what to expect. Below are some ***answer***s to frequently asked questions about online classes.

Ques. *Is an online class the same as a self-paced class?*

Answer: No. While some online classes are similar to independent study, most online classes are not self-paced classes. The due dates for documents and class participation reflect those of a "regular" campus class. Homework, other activities, and online class participation must be completed by preset dates and times.

Ques. *How much time do I have to spend online?*

Answer: You should plan to spend at least the same amount of time you would spend on a face-to-face class. And probably more, at least at first, as you get oriented to the online CMS.

Ques. *Do I have to log on to class at a particular time?*

Answer: No. You will have deadlines by which to post your work, but when you complete that work is upto you. You should try to do your work on a daily basis so as to avoid being overburdened at the end of each unit.

Ques. *Is taking a class online easier than a "regular" class?*

Answer: No. The course content in an online class is usually identical to that of a face-to-face class on the same topic. Some people think the workload is even more demanding than a regular face-to-face class in that you have to be a self-directed learner, stay motivated, and stay on top of your workload independently. It has been shown that the most successful online students/teachers tend to share the following characteristics:

- Self-motivation/self-starter
- Good organization and time-management skills
- Familiar with computers and the Internet
- Resourceful and actively seek answers and solutions to questions and problems

Ques. *What Internet skills would be helpful in an online class?*

Answer: The most successful students have the following Internet skills:

- Familiarity with Web browsers and an e-mail programme.
- Some familiarity with Web-based interactions, such as email, discussion boards, listservs, and chat rooms.
- Proficiency with typing and word processing.
- Experience in successful Internet searches using a variety of search engines.

Ques. How is online teaching different from traditional classroom teaching?

Answer: The online model emphasizes an interactive learning environment, designed to stimulate dialogue between instructor and students and among students themselves. The online process requires both instructor and students to take active roles. The instructor will often act as a facilitator, organizing activities that engage students directly rather than relying too heavily on lectures and memorization.

Ques. *When and where do classes take place?*

Answer: We don't really "meet" in a real-time or physical face-to-face sense. Instead, we interact regularly through the CMS and via email. Courses take place wherever your computer is: at home, at work, on the road-anywhere you can connect to the Internet. Courses are typically organized by week with specific due dates. The model is primarily asynchronous, which means that within each week you and your students may log in whenever it is most convenient. Generally, logging in four to five times per week is necessary to give timely feedback and interact sufficiently with students. Although communication is primarily asynchronous, real-time chat is also available.

Ques. *How will I be able to communicate with my students?*

Answer: A lot of instructors mistakenly assume that they'll feel isolated from their online students. To their surprise, most instructors find that online courses actually provide a high degree of personal contact, and many say that they get to know their online students much better than their students in on-ground courses. This is because asynchronous, online courses offer many more opportunities for reflection, in-depth discussion, and interaction than traditional courses that meet only once or twice a week. Not only will you and your students communicate directly, everyone in the class can be involved in group-and class-level discussions contributing as much and as often as they want. Far from being an impediment to communication, the online format facilitates and enhances communication and interaction in ways that would be impossible in other situations.

Ques. *What are some of the advantages of attending college online?*

Answer: Online education is known for its flexibility, but studies have identified several additional benefits of attending class online. Among them are

Communication: Many students are more comfortable engaging in meaningful discussions online than in a classroom. These students might have hearing or speech impairments; speak different languages; have severe social anxiety; or simply need more time to organize their thoughts.

Personalized learning: Not all students learn the same way. Web-based learning allows instructors to deliver the same content using different media, like videos or simulations, personalizing learning. Online classes providing round-the-clock access to materials and lectures also let students study when they feel most focussed and engaged.

Accessibility: Online programmes transcend time, geographic, and other barriers to higher education. This can be helpful for those who work full-time, live in remote regions, or serve in the military.

Adaptability: Learning management systems that integrate text-to-speech and other adaptive technologies support learners with physical, behavioural, and learning challenges.

Efficiency: Studies show online students tend to achieve the same learning results in half the time as classroom-based students.

Engagement: Online instructors can use games, social media, virtual badges, and other engaging technologies to motivate students and enhance learning.

Ques. *Can you really earn online degrees in hands-on fields like nursing and engineering?*

Answer: Yes and no. While schools do offer online and hybrid programmes in these disciplines, students must usually meet additional face-to-face training requirements. Schools usually establish these requirements with convenience in mind. For example, students in fields like nursing, teaching, and social work may be required to complete supervised fieldwork or clinical placements, but do so through local schools, hospitals/clinics, and other organizations. For example, students enrolled in the University of Virginia's Engineers produced in Virginia programme can complete all their engineering classes online in a live format while gaining practical experience through strategic internships with employers across the state.

Some online programmes do require students to complete on-campus training, seminars and assessments, but visits are often designed to minimize cost and travel. Students should consider these requirements when researching programmes.

Ques. *Is online education as effective as face-to-face instruction?*

Answer: Online education may seem relatively new, but years of research suggests it can be just as effective as traditional coursework, and often more so. According to a U.S. Department of Education analysis of more than 1,000 learning studies, online students tend to outperform classroom-based students across most disciplines and demographics. Another major review published the same year found that online students had the advantage 70 per cent of the time, a gap authors projected would only widen as programmes and technologies evolve.

While these reports list several plausible reasons, students might learn more effectively online—that they have more control over their studies, or more opportunities for reflection—medium is only one of many factors that influence outcomes. Successful online students tend to be organized self-starters who can complete their work without reporting to a traditional classroom. Learning styles and preferences matter, too. Prospective students should research programmes carefully to identify which ones offer the best chance of success.

Ques. *Do employers accept online degrees?*

Answer: All new learning innovations are met with some degree of scrutiny, but skepticism subsides as methods become more mainstream. Such is the case for online learning. Studies indicate employers who are familiar with online degrees tend to view them more favourably, and more employers are acquainted with them than ever before. The majority of colleges now offer online degrees, including most public, not-for-profit, and Ivy League universities. Online learning is also increasingly prevalent in the workplace as more companies invest in web-based employee training and development programmes.

Ques. *Is online education more conducive to cheating?*

Answer: The concern that online students cheat more than traditional students is perhaps misplaced. When researchers at Marshall University conducted a study to measure the prevalence of cheating in online and classroom-based courses, they concluded, "somewhat surprisingly, the results showed higher rates of academic dishonesty in live courses." The authors suggest the social familiarity of students in a classroom setting may lessen their sense of moral obligation.

Another reason cheating is less common in online programmes is that colleges have adopted strict anti-cheating protocols and technologies. According to a report published by the Online Learning Consortium, some online courses require students to report to proctored testing facilities to complete exams, though virtual proctoring using shared screens and webcams is increasingly popular. Sophisticated identity verification tools like biometric analysis and facial recognition software are another way these schools combat cheating. Instructors often implement their own anti-cheating measures, too, like running research papers through plagiarism-detection programmes or incorporating challenge-based questions in quizzes and exams. When combined, these measures can reduce academic dishonesty significantly.

In an interview with OnlineEducation.com, Dr. Susan Aldridge, president of Drexel University Online, discussed the overall approach many universities take to curbing cheating—an approach that includes both technical and policy-based prevention strategies.

"Like most online higher education providers, Drexel University employs a three-pronged approach to maintaining academic integrity among its virtual students," said Dr. Aldridge. "We create solid barriers to cheating, while also making every effort to identify and sanction it as it occurs or directly after the fact. At the same time, we foster a principled community of inquiry that, in turn, motivates students to act in ethical ways. So, with this triad in mind, we have implemented more than a few strategies and systems to ensure academic integrity."

Ques. *How do I know if online education is right for me?*

Answer: Choosing the right degree programme takes time and careful research no matter how one intends to study. Learning styles, goals, and programmes always vary, but students considering online colleges must consider technical skills, ability to self-motivate, and other factors specific to the medium. A number of colleges and universities have developed assessments to help prospective students determine whether they are prepared for online learning. You can access a compilation of assessments from many different colleges online. Online course demos and trials can also be helpful, particularly if they are offered by schools of interest. Students can call online colleges and ask to speak an admissions representative who can clarify additional requirements and expectations.

Ques. *How do I know if an online degree programme is credible?*

Answer: As with traditional colleges, some online schools are considered more credible than others. Reputation, post-graduation employment statistics, and enrollment numbers are not always reliable indicators of quality, which is why many experts advise students to look for accredited schools. In order for an online college to be accredited, a third-party organization must review its practices, finances, instructors, and other important criteria and certify that they meet certain quality standards. The certifying organization matters, too, since accreditation is only as reliable as the agency that grants it. Students should confirm online programmes' accrediting agencies are recognized by the U.S. Department of Education and/or the Council on Higher Education Accreditation before submitting their applications.

Ques. *Do online schools offer the same student support services as traditional colleges?*

Answer: Colleges and universities tend to offer online students many of the same support services as campus-based students, though they may be administered differently. Instead of going to a campus library, online students may log in to virtual libraries stocked with digital materials, or work with research librarians by phone or email. Tutoring, academic advising, and career services might rely on video conferencing software, virtual meeting rooms, and other collaborative technologies. Some online colleges offer non-academic student support services as well. For example, Western Governor University's Student Assistance Programme provides online students with 24/7 access to personal counselling, legal advice, and financial consulting services. A list of student support services is usually readily available on online colleges' websites.

Ques. *What technical skills do online students need?*

Answer: Online learning platforms are typically designed to be as user-friendly as possible: intuitive controls, clear instructions, and tutorials guide students through new tasks. However, students still need basic computer skills to access and navigate these programmes. These skills include: using a keyboard and a mouse; running computer programmes; using the Internet; sending and receiving email; using word processing programmes; and using forums and other collaborative tools. Most online programmes publish such requirements on their websites. If not, an admissions adviser can help.

Ques. *What technology requirements must online students meet? What if they do not meet them?*

Answer: Technical requirements vary from one online degree programme to the next, but most students need at minimum high-speed Internet access, a keyboard, and a computer capable of running specified online learning software. Courses using identity verification tools and voice-or web-conferencing software require webcams and microphones. Scanners and printers help, too. While online schools increasingly offer mobile apps for learning on-the-go, smartphones and tablets alone may not be sufficient.

Most online colleges list minimum technology requirements on their websites. Students who do not meet these requirements should contact schools directly to inquire about 'programmes that can help. Some online schools lend or provide laptops, netbooks, or tablets for little to no cost, though students must generally return them right away, if they withdraw from courses. Other colleges may offer grants and scholarships to help cover technical costs for students who qualify.

Ques. *Can students use military education benefits to pay for online education?*

Answer: Active-duty and veteran military service-members can typically apply their military education benefits toward an online degree, though they must still meet many of the same eligibility requirements detailed in the previous ***answer***. Many state-level benefits have additional residency requirements. Most colleges have whole offices dedicated to helping these students understand and use their benefits effectively. They may also clarify applicable aid programmes and requirements on their official websites. When in doubt, students should contact schools directly or report to the nearest Department of Veteran Affairs to learn more about their options.

Interesting Facts about Online Education in India

- Online education market in India was worth $ 247 million in 2016, which is expected to grow about $ 1.96 billion by 2021. That is a compound annual growth rate of 52 per cent.
- The number of users enrolled for various online learning courses is estimated to be 1.6 million in 2016, which is expected to grow about 9.6 million by the end of 2021.
- It is estimated that there is a 175 per cent increase in the cost of classroom education, this gives online education more preferred because it is cost effective.
- Nearly 48 per cent population in India between 15-40 age group with high aspirations but lower income is a good target market for online education. And, the acceptability of online channel is high in the younger demographic.

These factors clearly show the involvement and future potential of online education in India. Now let's discuss some of the advantages and disadvantages of online education over traditional education.

Technology in education is evolving at a lightning speed, aiding in making the learning more interactive and engaging also bridging the communication gap between teachers and students which usually occurs during the time of conventional teaching. In the past few years, the various type of technologies have emerged out in the education industry and enthusiastically embraced by multiple institutes in order to enhance student's skills and improve the institute productivity.

Now-a-days not only students but also working professional is running towards the online education platforms as it is easy to access the quality education and learning can be done at their own pace. As per the recent research report released by KPMG India and Google, named as Online Education. In India by 2021, the market of online education of paid users is expected to grow from 1.6 million to 9.6 million by 2021.

Growth Driving Factors

1. *Affordability:* Online education is much affordable compared to offline almost 53 per cent cheaper.
2. *Employability:* Industry relevant training can be acquired for the better jobs opportunity.
3. *Smartphone usage:* Expected to grow 180 million new smartphones users by 2021.
4. *Availability:* Beneficial for areas where the quality of offline education is low 10 million enrolments or expected by 2021.
5. *Government Initiatives:* Plans, such as Digital India helps enabling infrastructure needed for students to study online.
6. *Internet Penetration:* Nearly 735 million internet users are projected by 2021.
7. *Young Population:* 46 per cent population is young, higher acceptability of online channels.
8. *Disposable Income:* Expected to grow 55 per cent by 2020.

For competitive exams ways in which online education helps candidates prepare efficiently for different competitive examinations are as follows:

Webinar: A seminar conducted in the online mode is referred to as a webinar. These days many online players conduct webinars that help candidates in conceptual clarity.

Mock Tests: Mock tests are emerging as a popular course component for students, wherein they participate in a series of tests and get a comparative assessment (with other students) of their performance. With mock tests, candidates also get to know their areas of improvement as well as test pattern of the competitive exam they are planning to appear for.

Videos: Videos are helpful for candidates in solving exam papers and other problem areas.

Counselling: As a differentiator, players in online test prep market have also started offering course and career counselling services to students.

Popular Online Courses in India

Online MBA, Big Data & Business analytics, Digital marketing and Programming Remains the most popular courses learnt online by Indians. Here are some of the websites where you can learn above-mentioned courses online:

1. Online MBA in India:
   - Online MBA by ICFAI
   - Online MBA by Symbiosis
   - Online MBA by Indira Gandhi National Open University
   - Online MBA by Amity University
   - Online MBA by Sikkim Manipal University

2. Big Data and Business Analytics:
   - Big Data By Coursera
   - Big Data Courses by EdX
   - Big Data training tutorials by Lynda
   - Big Data Courses by Udemy
3. Digital Marketing:
   - Digital Marketing Course by NIIT
   - Digital Marketing and SEO by Digital Vidya
   - Digital Marketing by Manipal Global Education
   - Digital Marketing by AIMA
4. Programming Courses:
   - Computer programming by EdX
   - Free programming courses by Alison
   - Programming courses by Coursera
   - Online programming courses by Lynda
5. Web development and programming by Udemy

Online education in India has come a long way with the development of technology. India is one of the nations that is developing at an exponential rate in terms of technology. With the population of more than 1.3 billion, the availability of high-speed internet and smartphones, India has the most number of technologically driven persons. The rise of the internet has changed the way of life in India. People like to do everything online, they shop online, do business online, make friends online, learn online, etc. While eCommerce being the most significant online industry, Online education and learning stand right next to it. With the ever-increasing information available on the internet and the countless number of online courses many people in India prefer to learn online.

8
Electronic Learning

The term, *e-learning* came into regular use around 2000. '*e-learning*' term is ambiguous. It is commonly used but does not have common definition. It has different meanings to different people. Since the term is now in widespread use, it is worth pausing on the variety of meanings given to it. For Wikipedia, "*e-learning* is a general term that relates to all training that is delivered with the assistance of a computer". Others deny that the "e" stands for electronic and argue that it stands for concepts like evolving, everywhere, enhanced or extended. This leads them to a fuzzy definition of *e-learning* as "a learning environment supported by continuously evolving, collaborative process, focussed on increasing individual and organizational performance". It is also frequently being used interchangeably with term, such as onlin*e-learning*, virtual learning, distributed learning, web-based learning also open and distanc*e-learning*. Despite their unique attributes, each of these terms fundamentally refers to educational processes that utilize information and communication technology (ICT) to mediate asynchronous as well as synchronous learning and teaching activities. Indeed, with expectation of the conventional print based open and distance education, it can be argued that the emergence of *e-learning* is directly linked to the development of, and access to information and communication technology infrastructure. *e-learning* appears to be growing out of three directions:

(i) From within educational organizations, which have offered open and distanc*e-learning* programmes within in a single, dual or mixed mode.
(ii) From conventional educational institutions that have never been involved in open and distanc*e-learning*.
(iii) From the corporate sector, many of which are favouring *e-learning* over residential workshop based approaches to staff training and development.

Forces driving the growth and development of *e-learning* seems to include (Naidu, 2003):

- The increasing accessibility as well as the decreasing costs of information and communications technologies.

- The capacity of ICT to support and enrich conventional educational practices through resource-based learning and synchronous and asynchronous communication.
- The need for flexibility access to learning opportunities from distributed venues, such as the home, workplace, community centre, and the conventional educational institution.
- The demand from isolated and independent learners for more equitable access to educational opportunities and services.
- The belief among many educational institutions that the application of ICT will enable them to increase their share in an increasingly competitive educational market.
- The need, among educational institutions, to be seen to be "keeping up with the times" (with the 'integration of ICT') in order to attract the attention of parents, students and other funding donors.
- The belief and the expectation that online-learning will reduce costs and increase productivity and institutional efficiency.

History of e-learning

The term "*e-learning*" has only been in existence since 1999 when the word was first utilized at a CBT systems seminar. Other words also began to spring up in search of an accurate description such as "online-learning" and "virtual learning". However, the principles behind *e-learning* have been well documented throughout history, and there is even evidence which suggests that early forms of *e-learning* existed as far back as the 19th century.

Long before the internet was launched, distance courses were being offered to provide students with education on particular subjects or skills. In the 18402 s Isaac Pitman taught his pupils shorthand via correspondence. This form of symbolic writing was designed to improve writing speed and was popular amongst secretaries, journalists, and other individuals who did a great deal of note taking or writing. Pitman, who was a qualified teacher, was sent completed assignments by mail and he would then send his students more work to be finished using the same system.

In 1924, the first testing machine was invented. This device allowed students to test themselves. Then, in 1954, B.F. Skinner, a Harvard Professor, invented the "teaching machine", which enabled schools to administer programmed instruction to their students. It wasn't until 1960, however, that the first computer based training programme was introduced to the world. This computer-based training programme (or CBT programme) was known as PLATO-Programmed Logic for Automated Teaching Operations. It was originally designed for students attending the University of Illinois, but ended up being used in schools throughout the area.

The first online-learning systems were really only set up to deliver information to students but as we entered the 70s online-learning started to become more interactive. In Britain, the Open University was keen to take advantage of *e-learning*. Their system of education has always been primarily focussed on learning at a distance. In the past, course materials were delivered by post and correspondence with tutors was via mail. With the internet, the Open University began to offer a wider range of interactive educational experiences as well as faster correspondence with students via email, etc.

With the introduction of the computer and internet in the late 20th century, *elearning* tools and delivery methods expanded. The first MAC in the 1980's enabled individuals to have computers in their homes, making it easier for them to learn about particular subjects and develop certain skill sets. Then, in the following decade, virtual learning environments began to truly thrive, with people gaining access to a wealth of online information and *e-learning* opportunities.

By the early 90s, several schools had been set up that delivered courses online only, making the most of the internet and bringing education to people who wouldn't previously have been able to attend a college due to geographical or time constraints. Technological advancements also helped educational establishments reduce the costs of distanc*e-learning*, a saving that would also be passed on to the students-helping bring education to a wider audience.

In the 2000, businesses began using *e-learning* to train their employees. New and experienced workers alike now had the opportunity to improve upon their industry knowledge base and expand their skill sets. At home, individuals were granted access to programmes that offered them the ability to earn online degrees and enrich their lives through expanded knowledge.

Benefits of e-learning

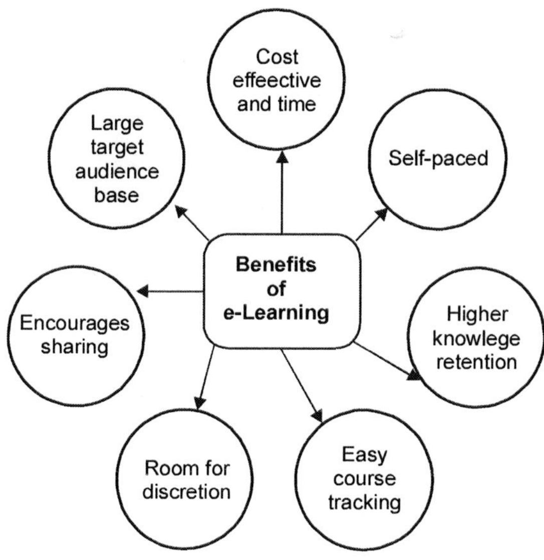

1. *It is cost-effective and saves time: e-learning* courses do not demand students to be present in the classroom necessarily. Students can proceed with the courses from the comfort of their homes or any place they deem convenient. This cuts down the money on travel and saves a lot of time.

Let's say an institute condenses 2900 hours of classroom training into:

- 600 hours of web-based training
- 500 hours of classroom training
- 300 hours of distance-learning

This cuts the time spent on the training by about 52 per cent. And the cost reduces considerably too. It is a win-win situation.

2. *The self-paced aspect of e-learning shines through all obstacles:* The best part about *e-learning* is that you can study whenever you want. Be it in the bus, the bookstore, the coffee shop, at home, on the run, or absolutely anywhere you want. And you can learn it at your own pace. With *e-learning*, there is no need to rush through your concepts and your understanding. If you hit a block, you can take a break and come back to it according to your own convenience. That is what self-paced learning is all about. Sounds fantastic, doesn't it?

3. *e-learning results in a higher knowledge retention:* To make education interactive and interesting, e-learning employs numerous methods of:

- Blended learning approach
- Gamification

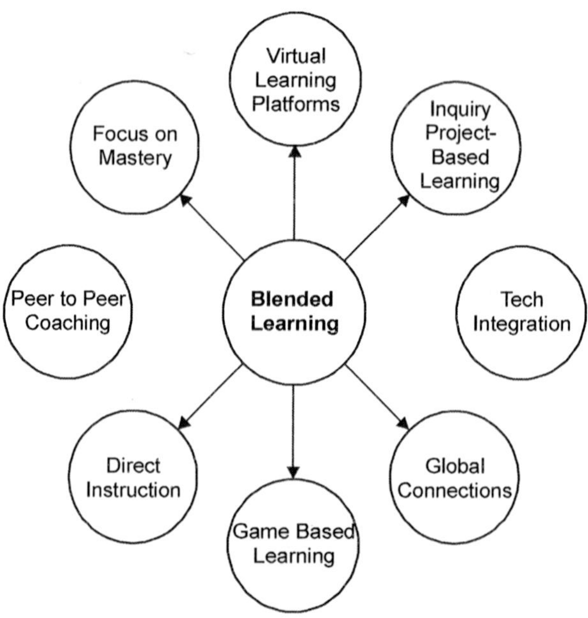

4. *Tracking Course Progress becomes Easier:* A well-implemented Learning Management System (LMS) makes tracking course progress more effective and easy. In addition, LMS makes assessing students' capabilities a piece of cake. Therefore, an ***e-learning*** system, which includes an LMS, can prove to be quite effective in tracking learner's progress.

5. *e-learning provides ample room to be discreet:* It so happens sometimes that a student lags behind in the class, while others find themselves quite in sync with whatever is being taught. And that student feels shy about questioning the incomprehensible, since that would shower him with unwanted attention. The whole situation ends up being extremely embarrassing. Such a situation can be completely avoided in *e-learning* and any failure can be kept from getting out in the open. Therefore, the chances of being jeered at can be reduced.

This appeals a lot to every student, mostly co-workers. So, these are what attract students to *e-learning*:

- *e-learning* allows enough room for students to manage their tasks as and when they find convenient.
- It also provides a step-by-step explanation procedure that caters to students of any level of comprehensive skills. *e-learning* takes personal learning to a whole new level.

6. *e-learning encourages sharing: e-learning:* provides students with a chance to share the knowledge acquired through online communities. A discussions forum can add value to th*e-learning* procedure, by incorporating scope for fruitful collaboration and conversation. Sharing of resources in *e-learning* is also an extremely healthy way for education to flourish.

7. *The target audience base for e-learning is quite large:* The two important aspects that act as barriers to learning are:

- Location
- Time-frame

This limits the student base considerably. With ***e-learning***, educators have access to a wide base of students, since distance isn't a hindrance anymore.

Did you know?

It's quite clear that *e-learning* is eco-friendly.

In a study conducted by the Open University, it was revealed that distanc*e-learning* courses consumed 90 per cent less energy and resulted in 85 per cent lesser emission of carbon dioxide per student!

Limitations of *e-learning*

- *Computer literacy and access to equipment:* One of the big limitations of *e-learning* that a trainer/student should be computer literate he/she should know computer. If student/trainer doesn't know computer he/she is unable to learn from *E-learning* method.

- *Some topics are not appropriate for E-learning:* Topics that require physical exertion and practice, such as sports and public speaking, are covered in *e-learning*. However, *e-learning* can be *a* useful companion to traditional education for teaching background and technical information.
- *Students themselves can be a limitation to E-learning:* A student who studies on ***e-learning*** programme should be self-motivated and discipline because no one is there to say is concentrated on your study.

Advantages of *e-learning*

Expanding E-Learning: The rapid increase in internet connectivity has been an important catalyst for the growth of *e-learning* A robust internet ecosystem, with a multitude of local and global players, will help onlin*e-learning* make further inroads The story is not limited to schools alone. Indian companies are adopting *e-learning* platforms as continuous employe*e-learning* has become *a* strategic necessity.

Unique Advantages: e-learning brings unique advantages, the prominent being the ability to provide personalized attent1on to all students in a conventional set-up, this is only possible when a highly skilled tutor offers one-to-one tutorials. However, considering that most institutions have a classroom-based set-up, such attention becomes difficult. Another advantage is people living in smaller towns and cities can get access to the best possibl*e-learning* resources from across the world, at a very affordable price. This helps create a level-playing field.

Live instruction: Certain curricula may require specialized instructors. By using live broadcasts, these instructors can remain in one location and provide instruction to many students in other locations. This type of specialization increases as students move into higher levels of education, for example, towards advanced degrees in medicine.

Video content delivery: Pre-recorded content, such as lectures, documentaries and other video content may be delivered 1n a store and forward model so that the material can be viewed, when needed.

Student-to-student interactions (video-conferencing): Students may learn just as much from each other, as they do from teachers. So, communications technology can be used to connect students.

Remote test administration: In some countries, standardized tests are used to evaluate students on a level-playing field. These tests must be delivered securely and on-time to meet testing schedules. In Indonesia, this is a daunting task simply because of geography and population size. Digital delivery could be the solution.

Up-to-date materials: Basics seldom change. However, virtually all textbooks must be updated. Textbooks are expensive to purchase, maintain and deliver. Digital delivery solves this issue when coupled with e-readers

Self-learning: Computer-based training or self-paced learning is common in higher education and trade-oriented learning Kiosks to support this may be located close to under-served areas where populations already work.

Business opportunity: In underdeveloped and developing countries, *e-learning* raises the level of education, literacy and economic development.

This is especially true for countries where technical education is expensive, Opportunities are limited and economic disparities exist.

Some Other Advantages

- Educators can experiment in creative ways using unique and intriguing websites.
- Remote delivery of cost-efficient and conveniently distributed "virtual courses"
- Networked learning gives not only education but also fun as students browse Internet in teams or on their own.
- Better performance and evaluation can result.
- Adopting new learning technologies in courses and curricula.
- One can become a part of worldwide movement of researchers.
- Better funding resources for technology research.
- New technology leads to more cross-discipline research and applications.
- Avoidance of obsolescence teaching.
- Learning can be more contextual as one can create interactive and animated hypermedia graphics and simulations that bring students closer to realities and experiences.

Challenges Faced

Even though the concept of *e-learning* is set to create major waves in the education sector in the recent years, the challenges are streaming in. Many organizations

have embraced *e-learning* with open arms, but the problems amount to a staggering sky-high heap, when it comes to implementing *e-learning* at the school level.

Let's shed some light on the challenges faced.

1. *The Internet is still a luxury in many parts of the country.* A vast majority of the Indian population resides in rural areas. The lack of infrastructure in such areas gives rise to connectivity and accessibility issues. However, the Government of India has been instrumental in removing such barriers by implementing various measures. Two schemes have been launched to aid in ***e-learning*** implementation:

- National Mission on Education through Information and Communication Technology (NMEICT)
- National Programme on Technology Enhanced Learning

These two schemes have been solely launched to implement ICT in video and web-based learning.

2. *e-learning does not cover a lot of certification courses:* The certifications that come with conventional learning is somehow lost in the *e-learning* concept of education. The *e-learning* courses do not cover a lot of certification courses that are recognized by colleges and universities across India or abroad. This pulls the *e-learning* courses out of sync with any stream of school education.

3. *It would take some time to renovate the conventional educational system.* The traditional education methods have enlightened generations for decades now. Even though you might feel that they have overstayed their welcome, it has become increasingly difficult for us to overthrow tradition completely and embrace newer methods of learning with open arms.

However, renovation in the old-school methods have seen the light of the day with technology entering the industry. But a complete makeover in education with the *e-learning* methods would still require some time to establish itself.

4. *Not all learners are tech-savvy.* Even though the *e-learning* courses are available in a wide range of platforms for learners to choose from, a basic knowledge of how to operate those devices is imperative to benefit from the courses. And being a tech-savvy teacher becomes a primary requisite. Therefore, before *e-learning* could be implemented, learners and educators need to be educated about the ins and outs of technology to facilitate a smooth learning curve.

5. *Lack of awareness.* If a large part of the population isn't aware of the amazing benefits that *e-learning* has to offer, then how can it be expected to change the face of education in the coming years?

Awareness plays a key role in making the proliferation of *e-learning* a joy ride. With that lacking, the future becomes questionable.

While the challenges pose an impending storm rocking the *e-learning* ship violently, the numerous benefits calm the waves to a soothing cradle. *e-learning* streams in like a shining ray of hope, making education accessible for:

- Anyone
- Anywhere
- Anytime

How to make *e-learning* more effective?

Provision of the men points will improve ***e-learning*** effectively:

- Availability of hardware (particularly computers).
- Faster Internet connectivity/improved bandwidth.
- Improved software.
- Appropriate policies favouring *e-learning.*
- Provision of technical support for *e-learning* at a range of scales.
- Lower prices for connectivity.
- Availability of reliable electricity.
- Appropriate content in appropriate languages.
- Awareness rising about the value of *e-learning.*
- Improved training for teachers in *e-learning* at all levels.

Important *E-Learning* Initiatives

India's vision of achieving full developed nation status by 2020 and of becoming a competitive player in the global knowledge based economy has made an integration of ICTs an absolute necessity. There is a further need for coordinated efforts from the government agencies and the content development industry to bring more creative innovations so as to keep pace with the growing trends and fast changing technology. Although e-Learning cannot replace the traditional classroom teaching, it can complement and provide quality and equitable education to every masses that are more neglected. Thus, it is worth noting the words of Bernard Lufkin's, the pioneer of "e-learning": "e" must be understood to have broad meaning. If '*e-learning*' is to be effective, then 'e' should be interpreted to mean exciting, energetic, enthusiastic, emotional, extended, excellent and educational in addition to 'Electronic'

Some Important e-Learning Initiatives in India

Realizing the importance of e-Learning, UGC. Organized a dialogue on "Enhancing Higher Education through e-Learning" in collaboration, with the Commonwealth of Learning (COL), Vancouver during 17-19 November, 2003 at New Delhi. The dialogue was attended by Vice Chancellors of some selected Indian universities, heads of UGC'S national centers, and experts from COL and outside India. One of the recommendations of the group was that UGC should create a system to support the use of e-Learning by all institutions of higher learning in India, in an ambitious timeframe to enhance quality higher education through e-Learning. The real impetus of *e-learning* came from the National Task Force on information Technology and Software Development constituted by the Prime Minister of India in 1998. The Task Force report presented the master plan that India has in place as long terms policy of capacity building of institutions, human resources development in IT related areas, and use of ICTs in education. The Indira Gandhi National Open University (IGNOU) responded to the recommendations of the Task Force with its Virtual Campus Initiatives (VCI) in 1998 since then a number of initiatives are in operation in the country (Mishra & Sharma, 2005).

In India, the first ever international Conference on e-learning "Vidyakash-2002 was held in Mumbai by NCST Under the Department of Information and Communities Technologies, Govt. of India. Since then several conferences, seminars and discussions have been organized. Several organizations in businesses and education have been taking initiatives in e-learning field. Computer Society of India, NASSCOM, CII, CDAC, Chambers of Commerce have taken the ***e-learning*** concept as an important agenda in many of their Seminars and Conferences:

- In the contemporary businesses world, competition is rising, and there is a need of practicing managers, businesses heads and executives to upgrade their knowledge and skill set to address the new global business paradigm. Looking to such needs, Indian Institute of Management, Ahmedabad (IIMA) has created a new initiative that delivers cutting edge management education in real time through Virtual Learning Programmes (Rajpal, 2008). Without leaving their current jobs, executives can now avail the opportunity to enhance their capabilities and skill sets with the premier knowledge delivery expertise. IIMA has tied up with NIIT imperia to extend its reach to the working executives through Virtual Learning Programmes delivered online. The programmes are carefully designed and structured to reflect the most relevant needs of industry. Each programme focusses on new developments and latest trends in managerial practices relevant to the current global practices.
- Symbiosis Centre for Health Care has successfully implemented e-learning and is offering post graduate course in Medico-Legal and Health Care Management. Using e-learning, doctors, nurses and other medical related professionals all over the globe are currently able to get their post graduate degree from the comfort of their own places. Rather than taking time away from their regular duties or work hours, they can continue with their education during non-working hours. The courses are designed to make doctors more aware of adapting the management theory into hospital system.
- Under the agreement, UC Berkeley and UC San Diego, as well as Carnage Mellon University, Cornell University, the State University of New York at Buffalo will encourage engineering faculty to spend a quarter or semester of their sabbatical at Amrita University in Tamil Nadu State. Amrita will extend use of its e-learning centre, making it possible to be beamed over Edusat, a satellite launched by ISRO to transmit educational programming to multiple educational institutions throughout India. Three

US research centres are partners to the agreement. The US universities in this agreement are first-tier engineering schools that can help offset the imbalance in the quality of professors in India's fastest growing colleges and universities. With the help of American Professors, these satellite courses will turn more students into top level engineers not just for India, but potentially for PhD programmes and businesses in the US as well.

- Monjee Institute of Management Studies, Mumbai tied up with a third party service provider (Hughes Escorts Communications Ltd) for transmission of live lectures through Hughes VSAT network. The class timings and pre-determined. The Institute Faculty is required to go to the Hughes studio and the programmes beamed live via satellite to around 35 Hughes centres across India. The students are required to go to the centre in their respective cities and attend the live lecture. The lecture schedules, faculty assignments and presentations, examination details and all other communication is done through the nmims.edu site. The students are expected to visit this site and keep in touch with themselves and the faculty through e-groups. Now, NMIMS offers a PG Diploma in General Management (part time course) and PG Diploma in Business Administration (full time course). NMIMS also undertakes company specific programmes in the e-learning mode (Yajnik, 2005).
- Sponsored by the commonwealth of Learning (COL) International Crops Research Institute for the Semi-Arial Tropics (ICRISATT), engaged various states agricultural and veterinary universities in India and introduced them to the concepts of using information technology in distance education to reach out to village communities for enhancing their rural livelihoods (Gerad, 2006). Now, several leading technology institutions like IIT Kanpur, IIT Bombay and IIITM Kerala have come forward to lend their technical expertise to create and maintain a grid of education and extension materials. Many of other agricultural and Veterinary Universities of several states in India have expressed their willingness to join this consortium and contribute-learning resources to the grid. The greater emphasis here is one using best practices for developing courses for eLearning and on the reusability of content created by one institute by many others. The web-based digital repository would eventually benefit the global agricultural community.
- BITS Virtual University is a supplement and not a replacement of the conventional distance-learning programme of BITS. The students of distance-learning can now access and also participate in an online video conference over IP and Interact with the BITS Faculty at their Pilani office or residence through the BITS Connect network at mutually convenient time. If a student has missed viewing a live lecture session, then the student can view the recorded version of lecture at time convenient to him. An attempt has also been made to provide to the student a feel of

laboratory environment through a virtual lab. Convenience of access has been provided through the Distance-learning Portal developed by BITS Pilani. At present the BITS Virtual University is restricted to a few specialized Master's level programmes. Plans are there in future to extend this mode to other programmes as well.

Some of the other lesser known e-learning initiatives in India are:

- The most talked about e-learning project is the NPTEL project. NPTEL (National Programme on Technology Enhanced Learning) was conceived in 1999 and funded by Ministry of Human Resource Development. Under the project, 7 _TS and 118C worked on Rs. 20.5 crore from 2003 to 2006 to create 112 video courses and 116 web courses. These courses are available to students, working professionals and colleges at virtually no cost or very low cost. These courses could not attract much interest.
- Another commercial successful initiative is MBA programmes conducted for working professionals, using satellite video technology, by 111_, XLRI, etc. This was done by these institutions using services provided by Hughes Net, Research Infocom and NHT Imperia.
- Sakshat portal from MHRD is another well-known e-Learning initiative modelled onlines of MIT OCW It has been designed and developed by IGNOU for MHRD, as a repository of e-Books, e-Journals, Digital Repository and other student relevant information.
- Another related initiative again from IGNOU is e-Gyankosh, another digital repository for learning resources. It has been developed with the objective of long term preservation of learning materials.
- Recently, the Government of India started National Mission on Education through ICT, which has two components, firstly content generation and secondly connectivity along with provision for institutions and learners. It plans to focus on appropriate pedagogy for e-learning, providing facility of performing experiments through virtual laboratories, online testing and certification, online availability of teachers to guide and mentor learners, utilization of EDUSAT and DTH platforms, training and empowerment of teachers to effectively use the new method of teaching-learning.
- NCTE has recently launched a new project for integrating technology in education the XPDITTE (Xelerated Professional Development in the Integration of Technology in Teacher Education) project in collaboration with Intel Teach Programme. The Intel Teach Programme is a globally acclaimed programme that is being implemented in 40 countries worldwide. It aims to help classroom teachers learn how best to use technology to improve teaching and learning. This collaborative project aims to provide professional development in technology integration to all teacher educators across the country.

- DELN ET (Developing Library Network) is a major e-resource sharing library network in South Asia. It networks more than 900 libraries in India and six other countries and offers access to about fifty lakh, records of books, journals, articles, etc. DELNET also provides Inter Library Loan for Books and Documents Delivery Services for journal articles to the member libraries within and outside the country.
- UGC-INFONET set up towards the end of 2004, provides electronic access to scholarly literature available over the internet in all areas of learning to the university sector in India.
- CEC, an inter-university centre of UGC offers scripting, an e-course in scripting for films and television. Tamil Virtual University promotes Tamil language, literature and culture internationally through the medium of internet-linked computers. The university offers quality Tamil education over the web.
- CDAC has launched e-Sikshak, an e-learning framework and is offering free computer courses in Telugu, a regional language over its portal.
- The Oversight Committee on the Implementation of New Reservation Policy in higher educational institutions has chosen this model to emulate. Sharing resources from NPTEL in the South, the Kerala Education Grid portal has been designed to increase and facilitate access to education resources by the educational community and to facilitate collaboration, sharing of knowledge and best practices to improve the quality of education and learning.
- Also, worth mentioning is Vartalaap, a computer based solution over a computer network that creates an environment modeled closely on real-world classroom
- In 2009, IGNOU signed a deal with Department of Information on Technology, Government of India to facilitate e-learning in east India's rural areas and optimize the use of technology to provide education in the region. This initiative would tie IGNOU's educational services to 1,00,000 Common Service Sundays of IT Department spread in the country, which provide weekly access to ICT and Internet to people from rural areas. e-Learning programmes that will be linked to the centers include IGNOUs certificate programmes in agriculture, rural development, farming practices, community radio, etc.
- Tamil Nadu Agricultural University, with a clear understanding of the potential as well as the need of the-learning as a way of university system, has taken a lead in integrating e-learning in all undergraduate programmes since 2003. It is the first and only agriculture university in India to go for Open Distance Llearning (ODL) programme at Diploma and Postgraduate level. It is using e-Learning portal to deliver content online for blended classroom learning for 12 undergraduate, 29 postgraduate programmes besides using it for e-delivery of distance learning programmes.

- M.S. Swaminathan Research Foundation in Chennai developed National Virtual Academy for Rural Prosperity comprising village knowledge centres and Village resource centres programmes, with several national and international partners. All centres are connected by ISRO uplink/downlink satellite. The main aim of the programme is to empower vulnerable people in order to make them better choices and advice a better control of their own development and to build skills and capacity of the rural poor with a view to enhancing livelihood opportunities. NVA uses different modern and traditional technologies, such as notice boards, wired and wireless public address systems, WIFI based video conferencing, satellite based video conferencing, offline CDs for both audio and video, etc.
- In 2009, the University of Madras launched distance education e-learning Centre and a network operating centre at the University's Institute of Distance Education at a cost of Rs. 13.50 crores.
- The School of Science and Technology of YCM Open University initiated Electronic Engineering Programme in: 1992. The school prepared Virtual Classroom Models (VCMs) for some the courses of the programme. CD bases pre-recorded VCMs from master trainers are provided to enhance and enrich the-learning in the distance mode. The school visualized, planned and implemented various strategies to cultivate the production of using web based technology and Internet.
- IGNOU offers a one year Postgraduate Diploma in e-learning. It aims at developing competencies in design, development, implementation and management of online programmes at all levels of education, including corporate training. The target of the programme includes teachers, trainers, training managers, instructional designers and course developers in schools, colleges, universities and business and industry.
- Jadavapur University started a new inter disciplinary Masters Course in Multimedia Development with the technological support of CDAC and CMC.
- Aligarah Muslim University worked on a project to provide online education with focus on industries.
- The much talked NHT Varsity offers training to 5,00,000 students annually across 33 countries.
- IIM Calcutta, a well-known management school-entered into strategic alliance with NIIT, to offer executive development programmes through virtual classrooms.
- GyanDarshan, an exclusive higher education TV channel to provide quality distance education by IGNOU is an effective e-Learning effort.
- IIT Kanpur developed in 2003 Brihaspati, an e-learning portal as an open source freeware supported by Ministry of Information and Communication Technologies, Government of India. Faculties used this platform to post the lecture notes, handouts, reference materials, etc on the internet for

supporting classroom. teaching. Over 75 universities and institutions across India are being benefitted by them.

e-Learning in India remains mixed with a plethora of issues. Some of these issues include: (a) lack of adequate human resources to power the spiraling upward growth, (b) lack of uniform e-learning standards and workplace practices. These concerns a part, government apathy has also bolstered fly-by-night e-learning entrepreneurs who eye quick bucks and increasingly deliver 'learning garbage' to a global clientele (Choudhary, 2005). Small vendors have set up e-learning business houses with partly investments-in the hope of getting a sizeable pie of the global e-learning business.

A sizeable segment of these street smart vendors eye the US 6 Learning market-given the current explosion in 6 Learning expenditure in US. The basic quality that behaves a standard e-learning company is absent in these companies. e-learning process are virtually absent in these companies. Unfortunate for the Indian eLearning industry, at an era of globalization and information revolution, Indian laws have failed to contain these IT laws. The state of e-Learning in India remains a serious concern for the industry (Choudhury, 2005).

Action Steps and Activities for Future

- It is important to develop a quality culture in the field of e-learning and education in general.
- An interdisciplinary quality research for education and e-learning must be established.
- Research and practice have to make sure that results are transferred and put into practice.
- Bench marking models need to be established and Indian e-learning material need to be bench marked across international models.
- Development of international accredited quality standards for e-learning.
- Wide diffusion of standards through application guidelines and easy-to-use-tools.
- Enhancements of future topics of e-learning: Flexibility and mobility of learning scenarios.
- Bundling of interest of companies and organizations and representation in international standardization committees and association.
- National level standards for characteristics and content presentations.
- Guidelines for learning environments and systems in order to provide an effective and reasonable-learning environment.
- Methods like metadata for more intelligent information discovery systems.
- Norms for evaluation and comparison of e-learning programmes and methods for their recognition and transfer from one institution to another.
- Development of learning technologies for educational modeling, competency based approaches within electronic learning environment and the uniformity through tools, etc.

Main Strengths of Indian *e-learning*

India has a major role to play in the international e-learning services industry. It is already one of the leading IT service provider countries, and it is now aiming to achieve the same position in the IT enabled services. The presence of world-class educational infrastructure and training professionals enables it to be one of the leading e-learning services providers in the world. On the domestic front, the government and private sectors have taken many e-learning initiatives. Though these initiatives have been met with a lot of enthusiasm and user acceptance, their commercial viability is still under consideration. The government has been taking some proactive measures in a regulatory and financial capacity to boost the elearning environment in India. Funds have been invested in setting up Internet kiosks in rural areas for the purpose of communication, which can be used for e-learning initiative as well and can help in-providing informal and vocational training as well as formal education. The main strengths of the Indian e-learning services industry are:

- English speaking, highly qualified and techno savvy manpower
- Safe Electronic Environment-Official recognition for Digital Signatures and e-transactions
- Lower costs of human capital when compared to developed countries
- Strong and buoyant domestic education industry that facilitates upgradation of skills and introduction of new products

Future Trends

Business-to-employee initiatives will address e-learning Companies can build BZE intranets or corporate portals to conduct business with employees, and provide them self-service for access to benefits, forms and information. BZE capabilities will become increasingly important tools for recruitment, retention, and employee-relationship management. Also, will reduce cost, save time for the company.

e-learning will extend to customer CRM initiatives might include customer education. Companies can use e-learning to introduce new products, educate customers in self-service techniques, and compare competitors' products and services. Simulation, gaming and interactivity will enrich e-learning: Research shows that student understanding and retention improves when they learn by experience. Technologies, such as collaboration, interactivity, modelling, simulations, virtual reality interfaces and gaming will help students experience the skill while being taught. There will never be enough of the right skills. Along with technologies and business practices, some skills are changing so quickly that they're outdated within a few months of introduction. In addition, the number and range of skills required of the average employee is increasing.

Government Initiatives

- NPTEL

- Virtual Labs
- Talk to a Teacher
- Spoken Tutorial
- Consortium for Educational Communication
- Digital Library Inflibnet
- Quantum-Nano Centre
- ERP Mission Brihaspati
- ISLERS
- OSCAR
- FOSSEE
- e-Kalpa
- Robotics for Education
- Pedagogy Project
- Virtual Learning Environment
- Text Transcription
- OSS for MathsEdu
- SOS Tools
- Integrated National Knowledge Network (iNKN)
- IGNOU e-learning initiatives
- NMEICT
- Sakshat Portal
- IIITM-K Initiatives
- EDUSAT (Educational Satellite)
- VTU e-learning Framework
- Initiatives taken by Jadavpur University

Non-Government Initiatives

- Liqvid e-learning
- NIIT: www.niit.com
- Educomp Solutions
- Everonn: www.everonn.com,
- Hughes Global Education: www.hugheseducation.com
- 24/7 Learning: www.24x7learning.com
- eAbyas Solutions: www.eabyas.in
- Enable Mobile Technologies Pvt Ltd (Enable M): www.enablem.com
- All India Management Association (AIMA): www.aima.in
- Talentedge: www.talentedge.in
- Amrita VishwaVidyapeetham
- GurukulOnline-learning Solution (http://www.gurukulonline.c0.in)
- SIFY, http://www.sifyelearning.com
- Net Varsity http://www.netvarsity.com
- WIPRO Technologies (http://www.wipro.com)

9
Mobile Learning

Mobile learning, also known as m-learning, is a new way to access learning content, using mobile learning support, with the help of mobile devices, a continuous access to learning process. This can be done using appliance like your phone, laptop or tablet. You can learn wherever and whenever you want! With the advent of mobile learning, educational systems are changing.

M-learning is convenient in that it is accessible from virtually anywhere. Sharing is almost instantaneous among everyone using the same content, which leads to the reception of instant feedback and tips. This highly active process has proven to increase exam scores from the fiftieth to the seventieth percentile, and cut the dropout rate in technical fields by 22 per cent. M-learning also brings strong portability by replacing books and notes with small devices, filled with tailored learning contents. M-learning has the added benefit of being cost effective, as the price of digital content on tablets is falling sharply compared to the traditional media (books, CD and DVD, etc.). One digital textbook, for instance, costs one-third to half the price of a paper textbook with zero marginal cost.

Value

Those who have used m-learning programmes and techniques have made the following value statements in favour of m-learning.

- It is important to bring new technology into the classroom.
- Devices used are more lightweight than books and PCs.
- Mobile learning can be used to diversify the types of learning activities students partake in (or a blended learning approach).
- Mobile learning supports the learning process rather than being integral to it.
- Mobile learning can be a useful add-on tool for students with special needs. However, for SMS and MMS, this might be dependent on the students' specific disabilities or difficulties involved.
- Mobile learning can be used as a 'hook' to re-engage disaffected youth.

- M-Learning can be designed to combine decision making in complex learning scenarios with formative scoring and assessment.

Characterization

- It can get access to information and educational experience faster than other media.
- It is supported by portable devices, its mobility makes it easy to use.
- Comparing to other methods of learning, the cost of M-learning is relatively low.
- Exchange of information can be encrypted or private.
- It is easy to access all kinds of information.

Aspects

Along with the development of m-learning, many theories about mobile educations are raised by researchers, major aspects are listed:

- Mobile learning is learning happens when technological tools mediates between the learner and knowledge.
- Mobile learning uses mobile technology.
- Mobile learning as a continuation of e-learning.
- Mobile learning as learning about the learner-centered: where the learner is mobile and not necessarily technology.

Challenges

1. Technical Challenges

- Connectivity and battery life.
- Screen size and key size.
- Meeting required bandwidth for nonstop/fast streaming.
- Number of file/asset formats supported by a specific device.
- Content security or copyright issue from authoring group.
- Multiple standards, multiple screen sizes, multiple operating systems.
- Re-working existing e-Learning materials for mobile platforms.
- Limited memory.
- Risk of sudden obsolescence.
- Security.
- Work/life balance.

2. Social and Educational Challenges

- Accessibility and cost barriers for end users: digital divide.
- How to assess learning outside the classroom.
- How to support learning across many contexts.
- Content's security or copyright infringement issues.

- Frequent changes in device models/technologies/functionality, etc.
- Developing an appropriate theory of learning for the mobile age.
- Conceptual differences between e-learning and m-learning.
- Design of technology to support a lifetime of learning.
- Tracking of results and proper use of this information.
- No restriction on learning time-table.
- Personal and private information and content.
- No demographic boundary.
- Disruption of students' personal and academic lives.
- Access to and use of the technology in developing countries.
- Risk of distraction.
- Mobile usage habits among different countries and regions.

Growth

Mobile learning is widely used in schools, workplaces, museums, cities and rural areas around the world. In comparison to traditional classroom pedagogical approaches, mobile learning allows widened opportunities for timing, location, accessibility and context of learning.

Current areas of growth include:

- Testing, surveys, job aids and just-in-time (JIT) learning
- Location-based and contextual learning
- Social-networked mobile learning
- Mobile educational gaming
- Delivering m-Learning to cellular phones using two way SMS messaging and voice-based CellCasting (podcasting to phones with interactive assessments)
- Cloud computer file storage

Some examples of m-learning in the Indian context:

Flipped classrooms: This is a new education delivery mechanism that is revolutionising the education sector across the world. Flipped classroom uses a combination of face-to-face content delivery and offline learning approach to take the learning experience to the next level. It involves mastering initial concepts of a subject offline by viewing lecture videos and then interacting with experts/teachers later for clarification of doubts and for the practice of advanced concepts like projects and practical sessions where face-to-face guidance is inevitable. The offline videos can be downloaded and viewed using mobile devices and live interactions with the teachers can be done using smartphones.

Another variant of flipped classrooms that could be a boon for the education sector in India is the concept of Massive Open Online Course (MOOC). MOOC is an open source model for delivering high quality learning content/courses online to anyone free of cost, with no specific restrictions on attendance, age, geographies and so on. Top global universities have already joined MOOC platforms or started their own MOOC initiatives. Together, they host thousands of courses. The response from Indian students and teachers for MOOC courses has been fantastic. Globally, Indians form the second-largest pool of students attending MOOC courses. Some of the leading MOOCs providers are Coursera, edX, and Khan Academy. Initiatives like MOOCs when coupled with their accessibility using mobile devices will definitely go a long way in providing high quality education anytime, anywhere to Indian masses who have been deprived of it for various reasons.

Game-based learning: Mobile games have always been a favourite pastime for people of all age groups. Game-based learning refers to the use of games as a mechanism for learning specific concepts. The advantage of game-based learning is its capability to grab and retain the interest and attention of the learner throughout the learning process. Several mobile applications for learning subjects like mathematics, English, and statistics already exist in the mobile application store. More such mobile games should be developed for subjects in all domains in order to make m-learning an interesting experience.

Personalised learning: When it comes to learning, people will have their own choice about the preferred mode of learning. For example, some learners would like to read and learn, whereas others would prefer to watch a video and learn a concept. With the advancement in the field of learning analytics, it is possible to display content in a preferred mode of learning for each learner. Learning analytics refers to the application of analytics to the data created by each learner to track their personal likes and dislikes with regard to various aspects like type, format, and depth of content coverage in the courses. This would go a long way in enhancing their learning experience.

Social learning: The use of Web 2.0 technologies like blogs and communities to facilitate learning by collaboration and sharing of knowledge is called social learning. Now-a-days, many social media networks like LinkedIn and Twitter have also contributed their share to learning by forming communities and conducting Q&A sessions with experts in various domains. The most prominent usage of smartphones is for accessing social media networks. Support for learning provided by the social media networks will go a long way in promoting social learning using mobile devices.

The government has already taken some initiatives to popularise m-learning in India like the distribution of Aakash tablets to college students. However, these initiatives should be accelerated to ensure that the benefits of m-learning penetrate across the length and breadth of India and not only the student population. Some of the steps that could be taken by the government to promote widespread adoption of m-learning are:

- The government should offer subsidies to mobile service providers for providing special tariff plans for accessing education portals and specific education sites.

- Conduct m-learning promotion and awareness campaigns extensively in villages and other remote locations in India.

What could be the future of m-learning? Obviously, it will be something to do with the Internet of Things (IoT) ecosystem. IoT is a technology that is used to interconnect embedded objects/devices, such as sensors, mobile devices and so on, and facilitate communication among them without the need for any human intervention. The proliferation of IoT technology could lead to the emergence of wearable learning that is, getting custom learning experiences with the help of smart sensory and visual devices that obviously could take us to the next era of learning.

Potential and Challenges of M-Learning in Education System of India

Present Scenario of Internet Access In India

In 2001, there were about seven million Internet users in India. That number could cross 550 million in 2018 in the best case scenario, making it the second largest online population in the world. But without proper enabling conditions, the user base could only be 400 million in 2018, according to the 20 report India@Digital.Baharat by the Boston Consulting Group (BCG) and Internet and Mobile Marketing Association of India (IAMAI). According to findings of report on the Mckinsey Quarterly website Titled-Can India lead the mobile Internet revolution? Conducted by McKinsey & Company, following are the highlights of current picture of internet users in India:

- India has relatively few Internet users: just 7 per cent of its population is connected to the Web, compared with 32 per cent in China and 77 per cent in the United States.
- India's base of 81 million Internet users is the world's fourth largest. Yet this figure is a function of sheer population, not deep adoption: just 20 per cent of India's urban citizens are connected to the Internet, compared with 60 per cent in China.
- Even though typical Indian consumers have no Internet access, they have a remarkable appetite for digital content. In fact, they consume an average of 4.5 hours of it daily across offline channels, such as television, DVDs, and CDs.
- While India is a relatively poor country, more than 70 per cent of its urban consumers already spend about $1 a month on content and services through offline, unorganized retail channels—a market estimated to be worth more than $4 billion annually.
- The mobile Internet could deliver the personalized entertainment that Indian consumers crave. If India's latent demand is unleashed, McKinsey research forecasts that the total number of Internet users will increase more than fivefold, to 450 million, by 2015. Total digital-content

consumption will double, to as much as $9.5 billion. Including access charges, revenues from total digital consumption could increase fourfold, to $20 billion-twice the expected growth rate of China.

M-Learning as a Subset of e-Learning

Mobile learning is certainly not merely the conjunction of 'mobile' and learning; it has always implicitly meant mobile e-Learning and its history and development have to be understood as both a continuation of conventional e-Learning and a reaction to this conventional e-Learning and to its perceived inadequacies and limitations. It is the 'mobile' aspect of mobile learning that makes it stand apart from other types of learning, specifically designing learning experiences that exploit the opportunities that mobility can offer us. Many authors (e.g., Mostakhdemin-Hosseini and Tuimala, 2005) view Mobile Learning simply as the natural evolution of e-Learning, which completes a missing component such as the wireless feature, or as a new stage of distance and e-Learning (e.g., Georgiev, *et al.* 2004). M-Learning is often described as occupying a subspace within the e-Learning space, which is in turn a sub-part of digital learning. According to El-Hussein & Cronje (2010), the definition for m-learning contains three key components—mobility of technology, mobility of learners, and mobility of learning processes:

1. Mobility of technology-refers to the mobile nature of installed hardware and software that enable wireless Internet connection.
2. Mobility of learners-means learners are no longer physically attached to one or several learning sites, and they can be mobile and learn at the same time as long as the mobile devices are around.
3. Finally, mobility of learning is the result of mobility of both the technology and learners. If e-learning took learning away from the classroom or campus, then m-learning is taking learning away from a fixed point. Where e-learning is an alternative to classroom learning (actually e-Learning should/can be complementary to classroom learning)-m-learning is a complementary activity to both e-learning and traditional learning. M-learning respects that a user would like to interact with educational resources whilst away from their normal place of learning-classroom or computer.

Scope of M-Learning in Indian Education System

In India, most of the universities are teacher centric, where teachers decide the learning curriculum, lectures and other learning material. It is often found that what teachers deliver in class may not be properly received by students, the reasons may be-teacher may not be properly audible, the instructions delivered may not be satisfying, mode of communication or language is not proper or understood by student, shortage of time, students may not be attentive or do have a lack of depth on previous knowledge. In order to improve the quality of education, few institutions have added extra initiatives like e-learning as an aid to its regular class room study, but, as time passes by, it is seen that e-learning is being more confined to distance learning courses rather than as an aid to regular class room study. Institutions of higher education are always looking for effective teaching methods that place the student at the centre of learning. Keeping this in mind, universities are increasingly exploiting technology in the teaching they provide. The use of technology in higher education is based on the inter-relationships amongst at least three areas: technology, theories of learning and issues of educational practice. The increasing influence of globalization and the emerging information society, set new requirements for all areas of social life, including to higher education. M-Learning became an important instrument in the new Higher Educational Environment in the digital age which creates student-centred learning and educational practice, offering new more flexible learning methods. It enables connections and collaborations between individual participants and through their role as always-on, always-available, flexible personal communication devices. Following are some of the prospective initiatives in Education system in India to incorporate the advantages of m-learning: Flipped classrooms: This is a new education delivery mechanism that is revolutionising the education sector across the world.

M-Learning Challenges

Research indicates that m-learning offers considerable benefits to build and support creative, collaborative, and communicative learning environments. The implementation of efficient m-learning project, however, within educational environment is still a challenge due to the complex environment that incorporates management, pedagogical, technological elements, and socio-cultural issues. The following sections address and discuss some of the challenges imposed by the implementation of m-learning projects, these are: Management and Institutional Challenges; Integration to Technology Challenges; Technical Challenges; Design Challenges; Evaluation Challenges; Cultural and Social Challenges.

Management and institutional challenges: Managements of educational institutions need to define clear policies, and technical and pedagogical support, in order to go for wide scale implementation of m-learning. Lack of support and institutional policies were cited as institutional obstacles. One of the most crucial challenges facing the educational institutions, when implementing m-learning project, is managing the change within the institution. Managing such change will affect processes, activities, and components, as well as people, such as managers, decision-makers, content designers and developers, employees, students, and instructors, of the educational institution. The principles of change management have to be applied properly in order for the change process to succeed, starting with extensive and in advance planning. The goal of the change management is to change the attitudes and behaviours in the educational sector at different levels that includes different organizational and individual layers. Adopting a new m-learning strategy is a major change and naturally, people resist it, therefore, using the change management techniques will support moving towards the new era with confidence.

Integration to pedagogy challenges: It is challenging to properly integrate technology into their wider educational activities, and serious consideration must be given to teaching and learning strategies. The main drivers of innovation of m-learning should not be just deploying technology; there must be an integration of pedagogy and new methodologies that achieve educational goals. In order to develop successful mobile educational applications, design guidelines and new methods for the learning process must be followed, and, it is important to consider the methodological issues to develop appropriate pedagogical models. Significant efforts and steps have been made to provide methodologies and strategies in order to integrate mobile devices into teaching and learning practices. Dahlstrom and Bichsel urge researchers to look at pedagogical insights that will help instructors to better embrace mobile technologies. It is stressed by McGreal [28], that to accomplish this, mobile learning requires a successful integration between educational content and technology to achieve educational goals and to provide a successful teaching and learning environment. Alhazmi and Rahman argued that the technological features of mobile applications, such as mobility and interactivity are essential to successfully integrate this technology into wider educational settings.

Design challenges: It is important to understand that mobile devices are equipped with various features, such as: Camera, location, recording, sensors, search, media player, calculator, calendar, etc. Understanding these capabilities of mobile devices will help designers to explore the potential of mobile learning, which can truly support informal and social learning models. Designers of m-learning applications need to understand the three types of design, that is: instructional design, which is the educational design of the application; interface design, which is the transparent to the user; and screen design, which is the design of the graphics and the visual display. Al-Hunaiyyan pointed that the more emphasis the developer puts in these designs, the more useful and functional the application will be. It is essential for instructional designers to design e-learning courses effectively for mobile devices, he pointed out that m-learning should be viewed differently from that of e-Learning, due to mobile characteristics such as the screen size, screen orientation, mobile storage and memory, and network bandwidth.

On the other hand, user interface design is important factor for successful application. Thus, designing and developing an efficient educational interface within a learning environment is still a challenge for most developers, facilitators, and educators. Udell stated that useron:'s interface for mobile must be consistent and stressed to keep the application simple, when designing interfaces on mobile devices.

Technical challenges: Technical difficulties are a significant aspect in the implementation and integration of mlearning technologies in education. Qureshi *et al.* listed some of these difficulties which include "installation, availability of latest technology, fast Internet connection, and uninterrupted supply of electricity, maintenance, administration, security and absence of technical support". There are technical challenges related to the infrastructure, mobile device, application development, technical support, security, and technical knowledge of instructors, learners, and other stakeholders, which must be considered when employing m-learning project. These challenges resulted from the rapid change in technologies, programmes and devices. Furthermore, Park listed some technical limitations related to the physical attributes of mobile devices such as, small screen size; insufficient memory; limited battery; network reliability; excessive screen brightness outside; limitation of software applications; safety and privacy. In addition, connectivity and bandwidth need to be considered, when developing m-learning. Bakari *et al.* pointed that most of the developing countries lack quality and expert in technical support and maintenance of Information and Communication Technologies (ICT).

Evaluation challenges: Evaluation is an essential activity in the lifecycle of any interactive learning systems design, and mobile learning adds additional challenges for evaluation of both the technology and the learning outcome. There is a lack of evidence regarding the effective use of mobile learning in education, which he believes will limit the widespread adoption of mobile learning. Kukulska-Hulme and Traxler urged to integrate evaluation strategies into the development and implementations of m-learning technologies. Traxler said that evaluation of mobile learning is challenging. He identified some attributes that a 'good' evaluation should be: "Efficient (cost and time); Rigorous; Ethical; Proportionate; Consistent with the teaching and learning strategies; Aligned to the technology of learning; and Authentic". Furthermore, Park stressed on using various assessment methods of learners using mobile devices.

Cultural and social challenges: There are cultural norms and social concerns while accepting the deployment of m-learning. Kadirire and Guy pointed a drawback to mobile learning is the personal uses of the device with less control over the students makes mobile learning activities are subject to frequent interruptions. Ethical and practical implications, such as: resistance to change amongst lecturers; concerns about new social practices affecting lecturers personal time; increasing amount of information to be stored on his device; privacy issues; data security; and cyber-bullying, were addressed by. The accessibility of mobile devices is another challenge. If mobile learning is to be implemented successfully, students and instructors must own a mobile device.

McQuiggan noted the following as important factors that could determine the success of mobile learning:

Professional Development: Teachers, school leaders, school districts should be trained to use the technology effectively. The teaching programmes must make use of mobile learning and relevant pedagogies to train the teachers to be effective in the use of mobile technologies in classrooms.

Using data to personalize learning: Mobile devices allow novel ways to interpret data in form of logs and screen trackers which can be used by teachers to learn better about the students. Assessments and progress can be tracked in new ways and this can help the teacher provide a more personalized experience of learning for the students.

Changing instruction: Integrating mobile learning involves re-thinking about learning and usage of mobile phones. Adding apps to automate instruction will be of no use and have no impact in the long run.

Good content: Apps and contents must be aligned to the content taught in classrooms and should be localized to cater to contextual requirements for providing effective balance to mobile learning programmes (use of local language for assistance, cultural elements in storytelling and games, etc.)

By providing educational services using wireless and mobile technologies, educational institutions can potentially bring great convenience to those off-campus students who do not always have time to find Internet enabled computers to get important educational information from their academic institutions. With the M-educational services apps, students and instructors can access services any time and any place, they want.

10
Blended Learning

Blended learning is an approach to education that combines online educational materials and opportunities for interaction online with traditional place-based classroom methods. It requires the physical presence of both teacher and student, with some elements of student control over time, place, path, or pace. While students still attend "brated and-mortar" schools with a teacher present, face-to-face classroom practices are combined with computer-medining activities regarding content and delivery. Blended learning is also used in professional development and trend settings.

The terms "blended learning", "hybrid learning", "technology-mediated instruction", "web-enhanced instruction", and "mixed-mode instruction" are often used interchangeably in research literature. Although the concepts behind blended learning first developed in the 1960s, the formal terminology to describe it did not take its current form until the late 19905. One of the earliest uses of the term appears in a 1999 press release, in which the Interactive Learning Centre, an Atlanta-based education business, announced a change of name to EPIC Learning. The release mentions that "The Company currently operates 220 on-line courses, but will begin offering its Internet courseware using the company's Blended Learning methodology". The term "blended learning" was initially vague, encompassing a wide variety of technologies and pedagogical methods in varying combinations (some making no use of technology whatsoever). In 2002; me term became more concrete with the publication of the first Handbook of Blended Learning by Bonk and Graham. Graham challenged the breadth and ambiguity of the term's definition, and defined "blended learning systems" as learning systems that "combine face-to-face instruction with computer mediated instruction". In a report titled "Defining Blended Learning", researcher Norm Friesen suggests that, in its current form, blended learning "designates the range of possibilities presented by combining Internet and digital media with established classroom forms that require the physical co-presence of teacher and students".

Models

There is little consensus on the definition of blended learning. Some academic studies have suggested it is a redundant term. However, there are distinct blended learning models suggested by some researchers and educational think-tanks. These models include:

- *Face-to-face driver:* Where the teacher drives the instruction and augments with digital tools.
- *Rotation:* Students cycle through a schedule of independent online study and face-to-face classroom time.
- *Flex*: Most of the curriculum is delivered via a digital platform and teachers are available for face-to-face consultation and support.
- *Labs*: All of the curriculum is delivered via a digital platform but in a consistent physical location. Students usually take traditional classes in this model as well.
- *Self-blend:* Students choose to augment their traditional learning with online course work.
- *Online driver:* Students complete an entire course through an online platform with possible teacher check-ins. All curriculum and teaching is delivered via a digital platform and face-to-face meetings are scheduled or made available if necessary.

It is important to note that even blended learning models can be blended together and many implementations use some, many, or even all of these as dimensions of larger blended learning strategy. These models, for the most part, are not mutually exclusive.

There are many components that can comprise a blended learning model, including "instructor-delivered content, e-learning, webinars, conference calls, live or online sessions with instructors, and other media and events, for example, Facebook, e-mail, chat rooms, blogs, podcasting, Twitter, YouTube, Skype and web boards".

Prerequisites

Implementing blended learning is a difficult task. It needs change of attitudes of all those actors in the education system of the country. For implementing blended learning, the following are the basic requirements:

1. Well-trained teachers
2. Teachers with scientific perspective
3. Teachers with positive outlook and approach towards change
4. All the required facilities and infrastructures at the institutes
5. Awareness among the parents of students
6. Formative evaluation and continues internal assessment

Key Success Factors

Stacey and Gerbic identified several institutional, faculty, student and pedagogic variables that play an important role in ensuring successful blended learning experience. The Table below summarises such key factors along with their supporting references.

Key success factors for blended learning

Institutional	*Faculty-related*	*Student-related*	*Pedagogy-related*
• Respond to local, community or organizational needs • Institutional practice of regular evaluation • Building blocks include organizational readiness, technical resources, motivated faculty, and feedback channel • A transformative redesign process, rather than merely adding on technology	• Need for continuing professional development of teachers • Ongoing support through membership of a community of practice • Creation of shareable and reusable digital resources to help manage teachers' workloads	• Need to develop time management and virtual learning skills of students • Regular and open communication on learning expectations that students are required to meet e.g. online participation in discussion forms • Maturity and readiness of students for independent learning	• Pedagogical framework mapping different media to various phases of the course • Face-to-face feedback to students on online participation, to "legitimize" the latter as part of the Course • Integration between the online and face-to-face environments through a sequence of activities before, during, after and in preparation for face-to-face activities

Main Feature of Blended Learning

Lalima and Kiran Lata of Lucknow University listed the main charactistic of Blended Learning as follows:

1. Students have the option of the two modes
2. Teachers are well-versed with both the modes
3. Students get face to face interaction as well they interact in virtual space
4. Students get full experience in using new technology
5. Students get training in different life-skills
6. All round development of personality

7. Physical development is possible within school
8. Students get wide exposure and new perspectives of the course content
9. It has a human touch
10. It provides multicultural and multi-dimension approach to teaching learning process
11. Makes teaching learning process child
12. Diverse role of teacher
13. Student constructs knowledge rather than just consuming

Facts of Blended Learning

1. Face to face teaching
2. Student interaction with course content
3. Peer group interaction
4. Group discussion and exchange of ideas
5. Accessing e-library
6. Virtual classroom
7. Online assessment
8. e-tuitions
9. Accessing and maintaining educational blogs
10. Webinars
11. Viewing expert lectures in YouTube
12. Online learning through videos and audios
13. Virtual laboratories

Advantages

Blended instruction is reportedly more effective than purely face-to-face or purely online classes. Blended learning methods can also result in high levels of student achievement more effective than face-to-face learning. By using a combination of digital instruction and one-on-one face time, students can work on their own with new concepts which frees teachers up to circulate and support individual students who may need individualized attention. Proponents of blended learning argue that incorporating the "asynchronous Internet communication technology" into higher education courses serves to facilitate a simultaneous independent and collaborative learning experience". This incorporation is a major contributor to student satisfaction and success in such courses.

Blended learning also have the potential to reduce educational expenses, although some dispute that blended learning is inherently less expensive than traditional classroom learning. Blended learning can lower costs by putting classrooms in the online space and it essentially replaces pricey textbooks with electronic devices that students often bring themselves to class. E textbooks, which can be accessed digitally, may also help to drive down textbook budgets. Proponents of blended learning cite the opportunity for data collection and customization of instruction and assessment as two major benefits of this approach. Blended learning allows for personalized education, replacing the model where a teacher stands in front of the classroom and everyone is expected to stay at the same pace. Blended learning allows students to work at their own pace, making sure they fully understand new concepts before moving on. A classroom environment that incorporates blended learning naturally requires learners to demonstrate more autonomy, self-regulation, and independence in order to succeed. If teachers offer a form of initial programme orientation before introducing blended learning strategies, it can better prepare students to feel confident navigating the different components and developing a stronger sense of independence.

Benefits of Blended Learning for India

1. India being a popular country, formal education system is unable to reach most of the economically and social wreakers sections of the society. The cost of better education is very high and can not reach the poor sections of society. Blended learning can help in this situation.
2. Technological development demands the education system to match it pace and correlate with it so that students are able to cope up with the fast changing market. Presently, this is not the scene. Blended learning can benefit the system.
3. Availability of competent teachers is a big problem in the country. Untrained teachers are not very competent. Blended learning is a best option as online learning can be a good substitute for incompetent teacher.
4. The conventional teacher based system does not stand the test of modern technology based teaching system. Blended learning provides variety of experience to the students. Blended learning is dynamic and become more purposeful.
5. Our constitutions provide the provision of fee and compulsory education for all the children up to age of 14 years but our system is not able to meet the goal. If our educational institutes implement blended learning, then it is possible to increase enrolment irrective of geographical disadvantages.
6. Development in global market demand efficiency and skill in employees. Blended learning will help student in mastering modern techques and life-skills.
7. Education can be promoted among special children by blended learning. ICT supported teaching would enhance the capabilities of physically disabled students.
8. Very few Indian higher education institutions are reaching the level of slandered institutions in the world. Blended learning-teaching would alter the present status.

Future Path

Implementing blended learning needs a full dedication on part of educational authorities and managements of educational institutes. It needs a well-planned design that include all from individuals top to bottom of the educational hierarchy. For preparing educational institutes for blended learning there is a need to increase educational budgets. Very important issue that has to be considered is development of right type of attitudes towards this ground-breaking concept in all those who are concerned with educational system. For changes in attitudes of parents, community, teachers and students awareness programmes, seminars, discussion forums should be organised. These can be utilized to make people aware about the benefits of blended learning so that a right mind set is prepared for its implementation. Teacher training programmes both in-service and pre-service have to be reoriented to prepare teachers for blended Learning system.

Blended Learning to some extent is the solution to problems prevailing in our educational system. If implemented in a well-planned, organised way with right type of attitudes, it can become the future of our educational system.

11
Open Educational Resources

There is no one, standard definition of Open Educational Resources. However, the following broad definition of OERs from OER Commons seems to be generally accepted by the community:

> Open Educational Resources (OER) are teaching and learning materials that are freely available online for everyone to use, whether you are an instructor, student or self-learner. Examples of OER include: full courses, course modules, syllabi, lectures, homework assignments, quizzes, lab and classroom activities, pedagogical materials, games, simulations, and many more resources contained in digital media collections from around the world.

OERs exist within a wider 'Open' movement and context, explored below.

Open Movement

A range of 'Open' philosophies and models have emerged during the 20th Century as a result of several different drivers and motivations—including sharing freely, preventing duplication, avoiding restrictive (Copyright) practices, promoting economic efficiencies and improving access to wide groups of stakeholders. Many of these have been driven by and created by communities that recognise the benefits to themselves, and sometimes to wider groups. Some of these are listed below:

- Open source (relating to business and technology)
- Open source software
- Open source hardware
- Open standards
- Open access (research)
- Open design
- Open knowledge
- Open data
- Open content

- Open courseware
- Open educational resources
- Open educational practice

Several of these 'movements' or 'philosophies' have been significant within the education community both in terms of research and learning & teaching (particularly educational technology). Whilst it is widely expected that sharing and openness would bring benefits to some stakeholders in the educational community, traditional cultures and practices, managerial approaches and processes, and perceived legal complexities have been identified as barriers to sharing both within and across institutions.

Whilst the terms 'Open content' and 'Open courseware' are sometimes used to mean the wide range of resources to support learning and teaching, one is fairly broad and the other very specific. We have chosen to use the term 'Open Educational Resources' (OER), as this relates to resources that are specifically licenced to be used and re-used in an educational context.

Educational Resources

Whilst purely informational content has a significant role in learning and teaching, it is helpful to consider learning resources by their levels of granularity and to focus on the degree to which information content is embedded within a learning activity:

- *Digital assets*—normally a single file (e.g. an image, video or audio clip), sometimes called a 'raw media asset';
- *Information objects*—a structured aggregation of digital assets, designed purely to present information;
- *Learning objects*—an aggregation of one or more digital assets which represents an educationally meaningful stand-alone unit;
- *Learning activities*—tasks involving interactions with information to attain a specific learning outcome;
- *Learning design*—structured sequences of information and activities to promote learning.

Open Educational Resources

The term 'Open Educational Resources' (OER) was first introduced at a conference hosted by UNESCO in 2000 and was promoted in the context of providing free access to educational resources on a global scale. As mentioned above, there is no authoritatively accredited definition for the term 'OER' at present, with the OECD preferring, '*digitised materials offered freely and openly for educators, students and self-learners to use and reuse for teaching, learning and research*'

OER initiatives aspire to provide open access to high-quality education resources on a global scale. From large institution-based or institution-supported initiatives to numerous small-scale activities, the number of OER related programmes and projects has been growing quickly within the past few years.

According to OECD in 2007, there are materials from more than 3000 open access courses (open courseware) currently available from over 300 universities worldwide:

- In the United States resources from thousands of courses have been made available by university-based projects, such as MIT Open Course Ware and Rice University's Connexions project:
- In China, materials from 750 courses have been made available by 222 university members of the China Open Resources for Education (CORE) Consortium.
- In Japan, resources from more than 400 courses have been made available by the 19 member universities of the Japanese OCW Consortium.
- In France, 800 educational resources from around 100 teaching units have been made available by the 11 member universities of the ParisTech OCW project.
- In Ireland, universities received government funding to build open access institutional repositories and to develop a federated harvesting and discovery service via a national portal. It is intended that this collaboration will be expanded to embrace all Irish research institutions.
- And in the UK, the Open University has released a range of its distance learning materials via the OpenLearn project and over 80 have released many resources which are used to support teaching in institutions and across a range of subject areas.

OERS in India: Present Scenario

India embraced OER by the year 2007, with support from government and external funding agencies. India is an active player in the OA movement with a large number of OA electronic journals, OA repositories and open source software-based digital repositories. Some of the open access initiatives have contributed largely to the creation, utilization and expansion of OER in India. These are as follows:

1. *Digital Library of India (http://http://www.dli.ernet.in//)* is a collaborative project of over 21 institutions in India and is currently hosted by IISc (Indian Institute of Science), Bangalore. It provides access to a digital collection of rare non-copyrighted books collected from various libraries in India. The project which was started in 2000, aims to archive all the significant literary, artistic and scientific works of mankind and to preserve digitally and make them available freely for every one over Internet for education, study, appreciation, and for future generations. It is also a partner to the Million Book project led by Carnegie Mellon University.

2. *National Digital Library (NDL) (http://www. ndl.iitkgp.ac.in//)* is an initiative of IIT Kharagpur and aims to provide free access to digitized educational

content in English and other Indian languages on a common platform. The project, started in 2015, and aims to bring under its fold 100 educational institutes and provide access to a collection of one million digitised books and journals in the first phase.

3. *National Knowledge Network (NKN) (http://nkn.gov.in/)* is an initiative that aims to connect all educational institutions, universities, research institutions, libraries, laboratories, healthcare, and agricultural institutions across the country through a high bandwidth network. Established in 2010, on the recommendations of the NKC (2007), it marks a step towards creation of a knowledge society.

4. *Shodhganga (http://shodhganga.inflibnet.ac.in/)* is a digital repository of Indian theses and dissertations, set up by INFLIBNET (Information and Library Network) Centre in 2010. This repository provides easy access to theses and dissertations submitted in Indian universities by doctoral and other research students.

5. *Vidyanidhi (http://http://eprints.uni-mysore.ac.in//)* This Open Access Institutional Repository, set up in April 2013, aims to cover scholarly publications covering journal articles, conference papers, books, book reviews, presentations, reports and patents since the establishment of the Varsity in 1916. The repository can be accessed by anybody, submission of documents to this archive is limited to the UoM research community. Interested users can freely download and use documents as most of them are directly accessible and full-texts downloadable, if the publication is in open access or if their institution has the accessibility to the concerned journal/publisher. 'Request Copy' forms can be used for documents to which direct full-text download is restricted due to publisher embargo.

6. *ShodhGangotri (http://shodhgangotri.inflibnet.ac.in/)* is a repository of Indian Research in Progress. This is an initiative by the INFLIBNET Centre which was started in 2011.

7. *EPrints@IISc (http://etd.ncsi.iisc.ernet.in/)* is the first open access digital repository, set up in 2001, by the National Centre for Scientific Information (NCSI) for providing access to research output by the IISc (Indian Institute of Science) research community.

A large number of initiatives aimed at promoting the use of ICT at all levels of education have been taken up. Premier educational institutions in the country have taken up collaborative initiatives for providing their educational resources through web portals. Majority of these initiatives are supported by the Government of India. Some of these are at a pilot stage while others are fully operational. Some of the major initiatives operating at a national level in educational institutions are as follows:

1. *National Programme on Technology:* Enhanced Learning (NPTEL) (http://nptel.ac.in/): This is a joint initiative of the seven Indian Institutes of Technology (IITs) (IIT, Bombay; IIT, Delhi; IIT, Guwahati; IIT, Kanpur; IIT, Kharagpur; IIT, Madras; and IIT, Roorkee) and the Indian Institute of Science (IISc). The project

was funded by Ministry of Human Resource Development (MHRD). It aims to enhance the quality of engineering education in the country by providing easy access to curriculum based video and web courses in engineering and sciences. Online web and video courses are provided for free, whereas certification programmes are offered for a nominal fee. The courses are modularised into core concepts and add-on topics. The materials are offered under a Creative Commons (CC BY-SA) license and are so designed that they can be customised for creating courses for varied contexts.

2. *Consortium for Educational Communication (CEC) (http://cec.nic.in/Pages/Home.aspx):* CEC is an inter-university centre set up by the University Grants Commission (UGC). CEC with the help of about 21 Educational Multimedia Research Centres (EMRCs) produces educational (audio/video/web-based) programmes on syllabus-based topics for dissemination through TV, Edusat, and Internet. These programmes are archived in a Learning Object Repository (LOR) and the Digital Video Repository (DVR) to provide easy access to these educational resources.

3. *Project Ekalavya (http://ekalavya.it.iitb.ac.in/):* This is an open source educational initiative by the Indian Institute of Technology, Bombay, for content development in Indian languages. It is an endeavour to provide an interactive platform for the creation, absorption, dissemination, and usage of knowledge. The project provides innovative channels of communication between the seekers and givers of knowledge. It is manifested in several programmes like e-Guru (providing online mentorship to engineering students), e-Outreach (repository of high quality educational material), ande-Content (proving quality content in Indian languages).

4. *Project OSCAR (Open Source Courseware Animations Repository) (http://oscar.iitb.ac.in/):* Project OSCAR is an initiative by Indian Institute of Technology, Bombay. It is a large repository of web-based, interactive animations and simulations, referred to as Learning Objects (LOs), for teaching various concepts in science and technology. LOs are on topics in various subjects at the Undergraduate and Postgraduate levels. The project also aims to provide training opportunities to students in developing LOs, managing the back-end of the repository, and conducting educational research.

5. *National Mission on Education using Information and Communication (NMEICT) (http://www.sakshat.ac.in/):* NMEICT was launched by the Ministry of Human Resource and Development (MHRD) in 2009. Its web portal is Sakshat-that provides one-stop access to e-content, e-journals and e-books. The aim is to leverage the potential of ICT, in providing high quality personalized and interactive knowledge modules over the internet/intranet for all the learners. All educational materials are offered under Creative Commons (CC-BY-SA) license.

6. *National Repository of Open Educational Resources (NROER)(http://nroer.gov.in/home/repository):* NROER, by Ministry of Human Resource and Development (MHRD) and Central Institute of Educational Technology (CIET), National Council of Educational Research and Training (NCERT), is a learning

repository for open educational resources. The repository provides a platform for creation and use of localised content available in variety of formats. The repository offers digital resources, such as videos, audio, interactive media, images, wiki pages, and documents, for all school subjects and grades in multiple languages. Content on the repository is released under a Creative Commons license.

7. *Agropedia (http://agropedia.iitk.ac.in/):* Agropedia is an online knowledge repository, serving as one-stop hub for information related to agriculture in India. The portal, designed as an agricultural Wikipedia provides localized content in multiple Indian languages. It hosts wide range of agricultural information organized in the form of knowledge objects (text, image, audio, and video), and knowledge models represented using concept mapping tools. The project is developed by IIT Kanpur in collaboration with a number of institutions, with support from by Government of India through the National Agricultural Innovation Project (NAIP) of the Indian Council of Agricultural Research (ICAR). The platform provides space for interactivity, sharing of best practices, news updates, and online library (gyandhara) with certified content.

8. e-GyanKosh is a knowledge repository to store, index, preserve, distribute, and share the digital learning resources developed by the ODL institutions in the country. This repository offers online access to around 3000 courses of IGNOU and 2,000 video lectures. The video programmes are provided through a YouTube channel established for e-GyanKosh. There is also a wiki for collaborative content generation.

9. *e-PG Pathshala Project (http://epgp.inflibnet.ac.in/):* This is an initiative of UGC for providing free access to standardized e-textbooks for postgraduate courses in different universities of the country. The project is taken up under NME-ICT and involves development of High quality, curriculum-based, interactive e-content in different subjects across all disciplines at postgraduate level.

10. *National Council of Educational Research and Training (NCERT) (http://www.ncert.nic.in/):* NCERT has made available school textbooks and reference books online through its website to ensure easy and free access by teachers and learners. The books are in Hindi, English and Urdu. The e-books are available as flipbooks and can also be downloaded on the mobile phones. The material is provided under copyright notice with restrictions on further distribution and re-use.

11. *National Institute of Open Schooling (NIOS) OER project (http://oer.nios.ac.in/):* NIOS has taken up an OER project for providing easy access to educational materials for Vocational programmes at the level of Secondary and Sr. Secondary (+2) levels. The project is carried out in partnership with state level institutions and organizations.

12. *SWAYAM (Study Webs of Active-Learning for Young Aspiring Minds):* Swayam platform is an initiative by MHRD, to provide free Massive Open On-line Courses (MOOCs) on all kinds of subjects. It is an Indian Open Source platform based on Open edX for providing blended MOOCs in native Indian languages.

Microsoft has been selected as the technical partner for the project. Online courses on SWAYAM platform shall be made available by various partner institutions identified by the National MOOCs coordinator. The project aims to launch 2,000 massive open online courses (MOOC) for over 30 million students this year.

In India, government, universities and research organisations have realized the usefulness of ORE in widening the access to higher education and for this they are making several efforts to promote it in the country. In India, there are not many initiatives for creating open educational tools and resources. Most of them are in the area of science and engineering. Some significant initiatives are the following:

1. Digital Library Initiatives
2. Open Course Initiatives
3. Open Access Journal Initiatives
4. Institutional Repoditors
5. Academic Initiatives

Further details of the above initiatives are given by T. Bansal, S. Chhabra and D. Joshi of Guru Gobind Singh Indraprasthra University.

1. a) CSR Explorations
   b) Cultural Heritage Digital Library in Hindi
   c) Digital Library of India
   d) In XIV hosted by Institute of Mathematical Sciences, Chennai
   e) Indian National Digital Library in Engineering Sciences and Technology (INDEST) consortium
   f) Kala sampada: Digital Library Recourses of India Cultural Heritage
   g) Vidyanidhi
   h) Vigyan Prasar Digital Library
2. a) CEC Learning object Repositors
   b) e-Gyan Kosh of IGNOU
   c) National Programme on Technology Enhanced Learning (NPTEL)
   d) Ekalavya of IIT Bombay
   e) e-Grid
   f) Brihaspati of IIT Kanpur
3. a) e-journals
   b) Indian Academic of Sciences published OA Journals
   c) INDMED @ NIC and MEDIND @ NIC: Biomedical Journals from India
4. Institutional Repositories, such as Electronic Theses and Dissertations of IISc, Digital Repository of IIT Bombay, D space at National Chemical Laboratory, etc.
5. a) Academic Initiatives, such as Catalysis Database
   b) Librarians' Digital Library
   c) Inter-University Consortium for Technology Enabled Flexible Education and Development at IGNOU

Challenges to OER in India

The appropriate use of information technology can help equalize the distribution of high quality knowledge and educational opportunities for individuals, faculty, and institutions within India. However, there are obstacles to the spread of OER, which have been dealt in the following points:

Economic Issues: Teachers rarely show any interest in development of the open courseware as most of them are already unpaid and supporting the OER movement by developing the content at no cost is of no interest to them. Therefore, the concept of open courseware is encountering resistance from educators in India.

Intellectual property: Intellectual property is still the biggest problem with OER in India. None of the content is available under Creative Common License so as to ensure the copyright. In this competitive age, universities are seeking ways to protect their intellectual property for fear that it might be stolen or used by others and without assurance of copyright they feel reluctant to share thesis/ dissertations on public portals.

Infrastructure: Where there is shortage of power, it is difficult to imagine a strong network enabled infrastructure. Most of Indian semi-urban and rural areas are still struggling for sufficient amount of supply of electricity and the students in these areas are deployed of facilities being offered by ICT at their footstep. A strong network enabled delivery infrastructure with the focus on access and delivery is required to make OER movement successful.

Lack of Awareness: In India, there is still lot of unawareness about the availability of Open Educational Resources and the opportunities provided by them among the educators and learners communities. Libraries and librarians are still to get involved in OER related work.

Technological Backwardness: OER movement in India needs technological overhauls. OERs are presently based on Web 1.0 tools, whereas migration towards Web 2.0 is necessary. It is not just technological backwardness but may be non-affordability of latest technology.

Language and/or cultural barriers: Most of the OERs available only in English, limiting their usefulness to non-English speakers. Additionally, not all resources are culturally appropriate for all audiences. The Indian learner audience is generally from the non-English background.

Lack of Quality Assessment and Assurance Provisions: Most of the OERs are not following any pre-determined standards and are not related to teaching learning process. Moreover, the content is not updated regularly.

Financial limitations: Institutions are generally operating in a financial crunch. Since OER generally do not generate any type of payment for their usage, there may be little incentive for institutions to update their OER or ensure that it will continue to be available online.

Recommendations for Overcoming Challenges to OER in Indian Higher Education

There need to be considerable efforts in both directions-for reducing barriers and also understanding and stimulating use. Barriers can be reduced by dealing with technology issues and understanding can be promoted with R&D, feasibility studies, plus awareness creation. Following measures can be taken to overcome hindrances caused in the way of OER in Indian Higher Education:

- Development of user friendly system is required for ensuring the implementation for quality assurance of courseware;
- Adoption of new and appropriate technologies to match the teaching-learning environment;
- Initiating steps to increase the awareness among the teachers, researchers and students about the availability and benefits of OERs in facilitating quality teaching learning process;
- Reward system should be introduced to motivate the educators for developing open educational resources;
- Integrate OER into university curricula and organizational structures;
- Application of licensing, copyright and intellectual property rights;
- Modularizing the content to meet localization needs;
- Development of skills among the teachers to use or share the resources developed by other teachers or institutions;
- High quality content materials can be achieved largely by funding content development from well established educational institutions;
- Capacity building efforts need to be made for both teachers and learners to train them for effective use of OER;
- Research should be increased in about and around OER so as to make future efforts in the right direction;
- Infrastructure needs to be developed for general software and middleware services for creating, federating, and finding OER resources;
- Appropriate e-infrastructure or cyber infrastructure needs to be generated in the country;

Conclusion

The present world demands creativity and innovation from all of us. A culture of learning needs to be developed so as to equip people to prosper in a rapidly evolving, knowledge-based world. A computer-enhanced learning environment can help make the much needed transition from just 'knowing' to 'sharing'.

OER is a concept rooted in the belief that unrestricted access to education should be entitled to everybody. Through a common model of open licensing, OER allows anyone to access, customize, and share digitally published educational materials for free, with the end result of advancing teaching and learning worldwide. OER has limitless potential to expand knowledge among lifelong learners around the world. Believing in the capacity of OER, the reach and impact of open courseware needs to be extended by encouraging the adoption and adaptation of open educational materials around the world. In India, we are still in the nascent stages of using OER. However, there have been recommendations, for the Government, at different platforms for developing a national e-content and curriculum initiative. The e-content and curriculum initiative should initially focus on the rapid production and acquisition of content in high need areas like agriculture, teacher training, basic and applied sciences and engineering, technical education, liberal arts and social sciences, communication skills, ethics and values, public health, and high end skills including management. Our projects should not be copied or modelled on the lines of those developed in other countries. Our model should be based on our needs like multiplicity of languages and available resources. Also, more efforts would need to be made for 'Building Awareness, Voice, and Understanding' about the issue.

12
Massive Open Online Courses (MOOCs)

A massive open online courses (MOOC) is an online course aimed at unlimited participation and open access via the web. In addition to traditional course materials, such as filmed lectures, readings, and problem sets, many MOOCs provide interactive courses with user forums to support community interactions among students, professors, and teaching assistants (TAs), as well as immediate feedback to quick quizzes and assignments. MOOCs are a recent and widely researched development in distance education, first introduced in 2006 and emerged as a popular mode of learning in 2012.

Early MOOCS often emphasized open-access features, such as open licensing of content, structure and learning goals, to promote the reuse and remixing of resources. Some later MOOCS use closed licenses for their course materials while maintaining free access for students.

The first MOOCS emerged from the open educational resources (OER) movement, which was sparked by MIT Open Course Ware project. The OER movement was motivated from work by researchers who pointed out that class size and learning outcomes had no established connection, with Daniel Barwick's work being the most often-cited example. The term 'MOOC' was coined in 2008 by Dave Cormier of the University of Prince Edward Island in response to a course called *Connectivism and Connective Knowledge* (also known as CCK08). CCK08, which was led by George Siemens of Athabasca University and Stephen Downes of the National Research Council, consisted of 25 tuition-paying students in Extended Education at the University of Manitoba, as well as over 2200 online students from the general public who paid nothing. All course content was available through RSS feeds, and online students could participate through collaborative tools, including blog posts, threaded discussions in Moodle, and Second Life meetings Stephen Downes considers these so-called cMOOCs to be more "creative and dynamic" than the current xMOOCs, which he believes "resemble television shows or digital textbooks."

According to *The New York Times*, 2012 became "the year of the MOOC" as several well-financed providers, associated with top universities, emerged, including Coursera, Udacity, and edX.

Benefits

Improving access to higher education: MOOCS are regarded by many as an important tool to widen access to higher education (HE) for millions of people, including those in the developing world, and ultimately enhance their quality of life. MOOCs may be regarded as contributing to the democratisation of HE, not only locally or regionally but globally as well. MOOCs can help democratize content and make knowledge reachable for everyone. Students are able to access complete courses offered by universities all over the world, something previously unattainable. With the availability of affordable technologies, MOOCs increase access to an extraordinary number of courses offered by world-renowned institutions and teachers.

Providing an Affordable Alternative to Formal Education: The costs of tertiary education continue to increase because institutions tend to bundle too many services. With MOOCS, some of these services can be transferred to other suitable players in the public or private sector. MOOCs are for large numbers of participants, can be accessed by anyone anywhere as long as they have an Internet connection, are open to:

Sustainable Development Goals: MOOCS can be seen as a form of open education offered for free through online platforms. The (initial) philosophy of MOOCs is to open up quality Higher Education to a wider audience. As such, MOOCS are an important tool to achieve Goal 4 of the 2030 Agenda for Sustainable Development.

Offers a flexible learning schedule: Certain lectures, videos, and tests through MOOCs can be accessed at any time compared to scheduled class times. By allowing learners to complete their coursework in their own time, this provides flexibility to learners based on their own personal schedules.

Online collaboration: The learning environments of MOOCS make it easier for learners across the globe to work together on common goals. Instead of having to physically meet one another, online collaboration creates partnerships among learners. While time zones may have an effect on the hours that learners communicate, projects, assignments, and more can be completed to incorporate the skills and resources that different learners offer no matter where they are located.

Potential of MOOC in India

MOOC has a huge potential veiled in India. Recent years have seen tremendous hike in the enrolment by Indian students in MOOCs all over world. India is among the leading countries in terms of enrolments in courses offered by many popular MOOC providers including edX, Coursera, and Udacity.

India is second to US, which accounts for 27 per cent with 8,83,400 users of the edX learner base and 1.5 million registered users on Coursera from India, as of December 2016. The growth of the learner enrollment is evident from the fact that the number of learners increased from 11 per cent to 27 per cent in just one year for edX. Also, currently 1.6 million users with 112000 from India, are enrolled in Udacity's nanodegree (six-ten months) courses including web developer. data analyst, android developer, mobile game developer, etc. Though Udacity offer only paid courses since 2014, it announced scholarships for 500 students from India to pursue its Android nanodegree programme (priced at Rs.9,800 per month), showing their interest in Indian learners as a market space for MOOC.

Anant Agarwal, CEO, edX, said, "There is a lot of talent in India, but often there are not enough slots for qualified students in colleges, and not enough financial aid". A study in 2016, reveals that a mere 20 per cent of the country's engineering graduates are readily employable, and that over half (53 per cent) of arts, science and commerce graduates are unfit for employment [6]. So, MOOC is an eminent alternative for the learners in India to have access to higher education, and to improve quality of their education with online learning. Anant Agarwal says "I believe that India ultimately will be a much bigger market for MOOCS than the US".

MOOC Platforms in India

Many initiatives have been taken by the Indian government to provide and support concept of open education. Initially, the objective was to provide open resources in terms of repositories, libraries, educational media files, e-books, etc. These were made accessible for everybody. Some of the efforts in this direction started as National Digital Repository of IGNOU, Sakshat providing e-content, Shishya for XI-XII Standards by CBSE Board, and Vidya Vahini integrating IT into the curriculum of rural schools by providing interactive training and developmental communication. Most of these initiatives started with establishing dedicated department to make education reachable to many learners as much as possible. Some of the common names in this path are Education and Research Network (ERNET) connecting various colleges and schools by providing network connectivity; EDUSAT, a satellite launched for education in India. Consortium for Educational Communication (CBC), use the power of television to act as means of educational knowledge dissemination; Information and Library Network Centre (INFLIBNET) autonomous Inter-University Centre for connecting university libraries, also it has started several other programmes. These all are the initiatives towards open education and education with Information technology still MOOC was out of their reach.

Moreover, the idea of online courses came into play and India started to work for this. In 2013, government launched e-PG Pathshala run especially for postgraduate course and it is managed by INFLIBNET 0f UGC. It is more of a repository of e-content and assessment than a MOOC. Also, two more course providers are Apna Course and myBskool.com. both are run in India. But both of these are being run for profit and clearly, providing open education is not among their motives.

Therefore, government set off to offer online courses on developing their own platforms. Currently, in India only a handful of universities and institutes have the facilities to start or support such initiative. Some of these organization and their efforts are as follows:

a. NPTEL: NPTEL stands for National Programme on Technology Enhanced Learning. It is a project funded by MHRD, initiated in 2003. It is a joint initiative of seven Indian Institute of Technology (HTS) and Indian Institute of Science (IISC) for offering courses on engineering and science, initially. Now, NPTEL has started online course in computer science, electrical, mechanical, and ocean engineering; management; humanities, music etc. It offers free course with nominal fees for certification. Anybody from anywhere can join their course.

NPTEL uses the open-source technology for offering courses. The courses are powered by Google's open-source platform Course Builder that runs on App Engine and Compute Engine. Also, it offers course content mainly in video lectures prepared in a conventional classroom environment, while some may also use slides to share the content.

Already, NPTEL is the largest single repository of technical courses in the world in the streaming video format and with text meta data for videos, text transcription and subtitling, and possible conversions to all Indian languages. Initially, its courses were having a minimal interactivity and uneven quality, even then the courses ceased to attract a large number of learners. Currently, it is offering more than 1200 courses and is planning to launch 600 more courses on various topics for the period 2016-2020. With the new course, they are looking to operate like MOOC providers in the market by offerings lectures, assignments and tests.

b. *MooKIT*: MooKIT is a lightweight MOOC management system built entirely using open-source technologies by Indian Institute of Kanpur (IITK), in '2014. It is a powerful system that can be used to offer online courses at any scale, from micro to massive. It is designed to offer CMOOC (connectivist MOOC). It has been used in 15 courses with about 100,000 registered learners.

It is specially designed to solve the problem of dealing with low-bandwidth and low-computing power situations using existing MOOC platform. To solve the problem, MooKIT provides an indicator that shows current bandwidth of the connection, similar to the bars on a mobile phone. It gives a visual indication of bad connection to the learner and they can use other content delivery options that MooKIT provides for example, stream only audio and play it in sync with the slides, which is often very close to the video experience. If the bandwidth is still low for that even, learner can receive a call on the phone and listen to the audio from there using the calling control provided on the interface (shown in Fig. 2). This feature is very helpful for learners belong to rural areas not having smart phone, laptop, internet connectivity, high bandwidth. They just need a dumb or basic phone.

One more special feature of MooKIT is the support of a very powerful analytics interface. Along with the instructor, it also allows the learner to view their course activities, which is not commonly provided in any other platform.

It is built entirely using Open-source technologies, and the core engine runs on the MEAN stack that uses java script based technology, making it extremely scalable. It offers four types of solutions based on the requirement:

- MooKIT Standard: It is used to run a single course. It does not require local streaming of video, but YouTube videos can be used. Example, mooeonmooe.0rg.
- MooKIT Enterprise: It is suitable to run a large number of online courses. Users are a part of a portal and will be able to enroll in the courses they're interested in. Example, mooe4dev.org. and agmoocs.in.
- MooKIT Replicated: It is suitable for low bandwidth areas. by allowing the content to be cached on local Servers. The serves will sync periodically for updates.
- MooKIT Personal or Mobi-mooKIT: It can run on the devices with low computation and low storage capability as of mobile devices. It does not provide forum or social networking due to the device constraint.

Video lecture interface of mooKIT showing bandwidth, phone call, audio streaming control.

c. IIT Bombay X: IITBombayX is a non-profit MOOC platform developed by IIT Bombay using the open-source platform Open edX, in 2014. It was created with funding from National Mission on Education through Information and Communication Technology (NME-ICT), Ministry of Human Resource Development (MHRD), Government of India. Currently, it is offering 63 courses on different subjects from multiple disciplines. Some of the courses provided are as shown in.

d. SWAYAM: SWAYAM stands for "Study Webs of Active Learning for Young Aspiring Minds". It is a MOOC platform MOOC launched by the Ministry of Human Resource Development (MHRD), Government of India, to bind online and offline education together. It is started with an expectation of launching 2,000 courses, to make it largest course catalogue, among all provided so far. For SWAYAM an independent platform is developed.

Learners across the country can get credit for MOOC courses offered on SWAYAM, and they can get their credits transferred and recognized at the parent institution, that was not possible in conventional MOOC platforms. In a talk, Dr. Phatak (HTK) mentioned that the mostly the learner drop out from the course as they find the courses either advance or not suitable to help them in scoring good grades in their university exam. Therefore SWAYAM is a right effort of credits using the course that will definitely encourage the learners to complete the course and get their certificate. For SWAYAM, a credit framework has been finalized that would allow the transfer of credits between institutions. An academic institution in India can offer up to 2000 of its catalogue in a particular programme via SWAYAM.

Currently, SWAYAM offers the courses for school, certificate, diploma, undergraduate, and postgraduate. The responsibility of delivering courses is assigned to six institutes based on their type, such as NCERT and N108 for offering school education, IGNOU for out of school learners, CEC for under-graduate education, UGC for post-graduation education, NPTEL for engineering, and IIMB for management studies. Though much of the course content for SWAYAM is the same content that has already been created for NPTEL, which is to be re-purposed for SWAYAM. Also, the content or videos created for this platform will be available on a platform called e-Acharya that already hosts educational video content created by MHRD. So, SWAYAM is promoting the best use of the resources, which is already a very costly affair.

Techology Used

For offering MOOC, interested institutions have an option to go for self-hosted platforms, or use proprietary platform, such as, Coursera, Udacity.

When using self-hosted platform, the providers can choose to-1) develop their own MOOC platform as done by IITK by developing MoooKIT, or 2) use open-source platform available already.

Indian government always believes in promoting the use of existing open-source platform as their preference. These platforms may require modification and customization as per the needs. Currently, NPTEL and IITBX are live examples of such effortless using the open source technology.

A. Coursebuilder: NPTEL courses are run on *CourseBuilder*, which is an open-source platform created by Google in 2012. It ties together the software and technology Google used to build their Power Searching with Google online course. Anyone can offer their own courses using course builder platform.

The platform provides basic functionality for presenting course material, including learner activities and assessments and instructions for using other Google products to create a course community. It provides basic services, such as Google accounts, hangouts, friend circles, which could be used as the social networking feature, if implemented properly.

Yet, the platform does not incorporate social networking as such.

Course Builder is built on Google app engine. It is written in Python. It uses the Google app engine for hosting the web application and python for server side scripting. In 2013, Google announced to work with edX as a contributor to the open-source platform, Open edX. Since then, they are only providing maintenance for their previous platform; no futhure enhancement is done from then.

B. Drupal: MooKIT platform is developed using Drupal, an open-source Content Management System (CMS). Drupal is used as a back-end system for at least 1.5 per cent of all websites worldwide ranging from personal blogs to corporate, political, and government sites. It is also used for knowledge management and business collaboration.

Drupal base code is written in PHP and it provides the user various Drupal APIs to work with and implement any feature on their own, or use contributed modules, if the feature is already implemented. It is hosted on Apache Web Server as an application. Drupal has a massive support of around 6500 contributed modules which extend features provided by Drupal core.

For developing MooKIT, Drupal is used as the CMS, the core pant of the platform, on top of which various other modules and services are defined to allow the user accessing services of Drupal. These modules are written mainly in PHP and Java Script.

c. Open edX: IITBX is powered by the Open edX. It is an open-source release of edX platform in 2013. EdX is founded by Harvard University and Massachusetts Institute of Technology (MIT).

Open edX platform is being used by educational providers to host their own MOOCs, all over the world. Including MOOC, it can also used to host smaller classes and training, modules. Also, educators can extend the platform to build learning tools that precisely meet their needs, and developers can contribute new features to the Open edX platform, due to nature of its availability as an open-source. Currently, it being used by various ellite universities like, standford, and the organizations, such as microsoft, and two indian MOOCs, IITBX and

SWAYAM are also on the list. The complete list of its users is available at.

Open edX is almost entirely based on python with Django as the web framework. It is a web-based platform for creating, delivering, and analyzing online courses. It is designed and developed using the modular approach where, "LMS module" allowing learners to access course content, such as videos, textbooks, problems; and to check their progress in the course, delivered by the "CMS or Studio Module". These modules are designed for instructor to create course structure and add course content, including for learners, also manages the course schedule, course team, set grading policy. Moreover, Open edX allows the users to analyze their course by providing a specific module named "Insight". It supports best and most of the advance features for learners as well as the course providers.

d. SWAYAM: It is being run on an independent platform is created in cooperation with the Microsoft. This platform is in growing stage, so much of its details are not yet available.

Features of MOOC Platforms

During our study, we carefully analysed the platforms to be familiar with their features. Based on our understanding of studied platform, we have identified certain features of MOOC platform.

MOOC courses have a schedule with staring and end date. Also, there are some self-paced courses that do not have any time restriction to join a course and always available for enrolment. Self-paced courses are only 6 per cent all MOOCS offered.

All courses offered traditionally or in an online environment support a learning model. For example, a traditional course supports face-to-face learning, while in online learning as in MOOC, the instructions are delivered in the form of multimedia content. Sometimes, instead of using a single model of instruction delivery, mixed mode approach, also known as blended learning. It brings together online and face-to-face classroom components.

MOOC course is delivered via MOOC platform, which provides some specific feature. For example, for the native users of different origin belonging to various states/countries, not the content but the platform itself is provided in multiple languages.

Sometimes, the platform used for delivering course is available with its code for everyone, to be used or customized for offering their own MOOCS. So, anyone interested in offering MOOC can use the already existing, platforms that are either available for free as open-source or pay for proprietary that are closed platform not available to be repurposed. Indian government have the policy to promote the use of Open technologies.

Now-a-days, more users are accessing the courses via mobile devices including tablets, smart phone, than ever before. By considering the factor and for ease of the users, providers are offering the mobile applications for their MOOCs. Moreover, these applications can support multiple platforms, such as android and iOS, allowing the learners to use the mobile devices to get enrol, access to course content, and participate in all course activities.

Therefore, we have identified some of the features provided by the MOOC platform, which are as Follows:

- *Course Format*: Whether the platform delivers self-paced courses or scheduled course?
- *Learning Model*: Which learning model is supported by the platform, online or blended?
- *Number of Courses:* A platform is running at present.
- *Number of Users:* Already registered in any course of the platform.
- *Institutional Credits*: Whether other institution provides credit for courses completed on the MOOC platforms.
- *Platform Language:* What are the languages in which the platform is provided?
- *Mobile App*: Do the platform have an App?
- *App Platform:* For which platform, android and/or iOS the app is provided.

Challenges for MOOC in India

Some of the major concerns regarding the implementation of MOOCS in India are the lack of technological infrastructure, investment, diversified population, quality of courses, adoption of MOOC among learners and their acceptance by the academic institutions:

1) *Technological Infrastructure:* MOOC needs the high speed internet connections for accessing the content delivered in their courses. In a developing country like India, Internet and computers comes under luxury and their availability is confined mainly to the urban areas. Limited availability of requisite infrastructure to access MOOCS has confined the extensive spread of MOOCS. India needs to work towards providing a better Internet access for the country's population and provides worldwide connectivity.

2) *Investment:* Offering the MOOC is a costly affair that includes the cost of infrastructure, platforms, content creation, human resources and many more. In India, the institutions do not have many capitals to invest in such event, so it is not easy for an individual institution to offer such services. There is need of involvement from some authorities, who can invest in the process to support the education. Even Indian government needs to liberalize conventional regulations and restrictions and encourage public-private partnership for creating MOOCS In this country.

3) *Diversified Needs*: India is a widely diversified country having multicultural societies and different languages spoken. For acceptance of MOOC among the huge domain of audience, they need to agree upon a common language of speaking. English as this language accepted globally, again throws away a considerable amount of audience who do not possess the knowledge or adequate Huency in English. So, a switch over to mostly English based courses as offered via current MOOCS often discourages learner to continue their courses.

The courses should also be offered in some regional languages, which may be a tedious task and prone to loss of uniformity and quality. Therefore, language is one of the barriers for learners from Indian origin that need to be addressed by the MOOC providers in a more realistic way. Moreover, the challenge is to deliver the lecture, designing of the course material, and the platform itself, in a way that can be understood by all. Hence forth, the main motive should be to work in the direction which an minimize the existing differences amongst the learners.

4) *Adoption of MOOC* among learners: Generally, in MOOC courses the communication between a teacher and learner and among learner as well is in written form. It results in the lack of oral communication skills among the learners and to improve this, they need undergo a traditional programme. Also, watching the course videos of other content on a computer screen can make the learner feel isolated. Due to this, motivation of learner falls resulting in dropping out from the course. Moreover, the courses that require lab or hands-on training may not fulfill the purpose completely in online mode. Therefore, the challenge faced by MOOC could be adoption of technology by learners.

5) *Quality*: To create and deliver quality content in MOOC, quality of teachers and technical staff is required. India has huge vacancies of teachers not filled, compounded by 0infrastructure deficit as the absence of laboratories. Also, it may be possible that teachers are not technically sound to create course content using the tools.

Emerging initiatives internationally and nationally are working towards offering quality educational by providing their content as open resources, but some of them are constraint by the adoption policies of their country or organization. India should also need to leverage these initiatives as a readily available, economically viable source of quality content for adoption. Also, a national quality assessment framework to assess the quality and adoption of new approaches like, credit transfer, MOOC, integrated courses, etc., should be adopted along with teacher training, their performance-related appraisal and mid-term re-evaluation.

Conclusion

MOOC platforms amused globally for offering online course and India is no exception. There are various MOOC platforms that are being used in India for offering the courses, such as NPTEL, MooKIT, IITBX, and SWAYAM. Except the NPTEL, these are the new platforms having history of hardly 4 t0 5 years, while SWAYAM is launched very recently. Therefore, to set up a ground for understanding including theoretical as well as technical aspects, a discussion is provided about each of these platforms with their features. Also, while using these platforms, it is needed to understand their current state, popularity among learners, use of social media for referring, searched, etc. and several other parameters or features. For the purpose a comparative analysis is provided for these platforms using web analysis considering several parameters as mentioned. Furthermore, there are some issues that are faced while implementing MOOC in India. These challenges are mentioned here. Some of these issues are already addressed by SWAYAM, which is the most recent platform.

13

Study Webs of Active-learning for Young Aspiring Minds (SWAYAM)

SWAYAM is an indigenous developed IT platform, initiated by Government of India, which is instrumental for self-actualisation providing opportunities for a life-long learning.

The SWAYAM shall facilitate hosting of all the courses, taught in classrooms from 9th class till post-graduation and hundreds of courses covering virtually every course that is taught at the university/college/school level and these shall be offered by best of the teachers in India. The curriculum-based course contents shall also cover diverse disciplines, such as arts, science, commerce, performing arts, social sciences and humanities subjects, engineering, technology, law, medicine, agriculture, etc. in higher education domain.

Any person in the world can register a course on SWAYAM.

Learner can choose from hundreds of courses, virtually every course that is taught at the university/college/school level and these shall be offered by best of the teachers in India and elsewhere. More than 1,000 specially chosen teachers and lecturers from across the country have participated in preparing these courses.

MHRD has appointed nine National Coordinators viz. UGC, NPTEL, CEC, IGNOU, NCERT, NIOS, IIMB, NITTTR & AICTE which have been assigned a specific sector for preparation of online courses for SWAYAM.

The courses hosted on SWAYAM will be in 4 quadrants: (1) video lecture with multi-media, (2) specially prepared reading material that can be downloaded/printed (3) self-assess tests through tests and quizzes and (4) an online discussion forum for clearing the doubts. Steps have been taken to enrich the learning experience by using audio-video & multi-media and state of the art pedagogy/technology.

The courses delivered through SWAYAM are available free of cost to the learners, however, students wanting certifications shall be registered and offered a certificate on successful completion of the course, with a little fee. At the end of each course, there will be an assessment of the student through proctored examination and the marks/grades secured in this exam could be transferred to the academic record of the students.

The courses delivered through SWAYAM are accessible by any learner free of cost. However student having registered a course, having submitting the Assignments as per requirements of the course shall at the end of each course, be assessed through a proctored examination. A student having successfully completed the course shall get a Certificate that shall be issued by Host Institute. The marks/ grades secured in this proctored examination could be transferred to the academic record of the students from Host Institute.

UGC has already issued the UGC (Credit Framework for online learning courses through SWAYAM) Regulation, 2016 advising the Universities to identify courses where credits can be transferred on to the academic record of the students for courses done on SWAYAM.

In order to improve Gross Enrollment Ratio (GER), from 20 per cent at present to 30 per cent by 2020; Government of India has felt that conventional mode of education shall alone not be sufficient to achieve this goal and has decided to utilise ICT in a, big way, in education.

SWAYAM will provide one integrated platform and portal for online courses, using information and communication technology and covering all higher education subjects and skill sector courses to ensure that the every student in our country has access to the best quality of higher education at the affordable cost to all students across the country irrespective of geographical barriers.

The Cabinet Committee on Economics Affairs (CCEA) on January 2, 2009 has approved 'National Mission on Education through Information & Communication Technology' (NMEICT), a Centrally Sponsored Scheme, with an outlay of 4612 Crores, to leverage the potential of ICT for all learners in Higher Education Institutions in any-time, any-where mode. Through this mission it is intended to achieve composite goals of ensuring access with equity and excellence in higher education and bridging the digital divide that exist in our society today.

Through NMEICT, massive effort has been launched to create e-Content for all courses starting from Under Graduation to Post Graduation, NPTEL (for engineering), UGC (for non-engineering, post-graduation), CEC (for non-engineering graduation), NIOS (for school level). Most of this content is electronic, but does not have the specifications of MOOCS, which an interactive system. This content needs to be re-purposed into MOOCs pedagogy. Similarly, more content needs to be created to ensure that all courses from the School to PG level are available in the MOOCs format. Under NMEICT, NPTEL (a group of 7 IITs&IISc) has developed e-content in 23 Disciplines numbering 933 Courses, CEC has developed e-content in 20 Undergraduate sbjects and shall further be completing e-content in 57 subjects in four quadrants, further, UGC is completing e-content in 77 Post Graduation subjects, similarly other institutes are engaged in development of e-content.

As per 'Digital India' Initiative; Government of India is emphasising on the use of ICT for education in a big way. Ministry of HRD, has accordingly embarked on a major and new initiative called SWAYAM, which will provide one integrated platform and portal for online courses, using information and communication technology and covering all higher education subjects and skill sector courses to ensure that the every student in our country has a access to the best quality of higher education at the affordable cost.

Major Objectives

Major Objectives of the proposal are as follows: (i) Creation of content on courses from School Secondary level till Post Graduation, covering all disciplines, to be made available on the SWAYAM platform, (ii) Re-purposing of e-content courses already developed under INMEICT to fit into SWAYAM Pedagogy/Andragogy. (iii) Develop India MOOCs platform named as SWAYAM (Study Webs of Active learning for Young Aspiring Minds) for hosting and running thousands of courses simultaneously. (iv) Provide robust Internet Cloud (with CON) and sufficient bandwidth for concurrent viewings of 1 million users. (v) Conduct of examination and award of certificates to participants having successfully completed the course. vi) Provide recommendations to Institutions regarding implementation of Choice Based Credit System (CBCS) on SWAYAM Courses.

Outcomes

The anticipated outcomes of SWAYAM are: (i) Creation of fresh content on 600 courses from Secondary to all levels of Higher Education, in all disciplines. (ii) Re-purposing of e-content courses numbering 1400 already developed under NMEICT to fit into SWAYAM Pedagogy/Andragogy. (iii) Develop India MOOCs platform named as SWAYAM (Study Webs of Active-learning for Young Aspiring Minds) for hosting and running about 2000 courses and repeating it three times during a year. (iv) Provide robust Internet Cloud (with CDN) and sufficient bandwidth for concurrent viewings of 1 million users. (v) Conduct of examination and award of certificates to having successfully completed the course. vi. Provide recommendations to Institutions regarding implementation of Choice Based Credit System (CBCS) on SWAYAM Courses.

Scope

Scope of SWAYAM programme shall be: (1) Curriculum based course contents covering diverse disciplines, such as arts, science, commerce, performing arts, social sciences and humanities subjects, engineering, technology, law, medicine, agriculture, etc. in higher education domain (all courses would be certification-ready in their detailed offering) (2) School education (9-12 levels) modules and teacher training as well as teaching and learning aids to children of India to help them learn subjects for better preparedness for competitive examinations for admissions to professional degree programmes (3) Skill based courses which cover both post-higher secondary school skills that are presently the domain of polytechnics as well as industrial skills certified by the _sector skill councils of various Ministries (4) Advanced curriculum and professional certification under a unified scheme in higher education domain that can be tailored to meet the demands of choice based credit system (CBCE) currently being implemented in India. (5) Curricula and courses that can meet the needs of life-long learners of Indian citizens in India and abroad. All course contents will have clear and designated outcomes for learners and follow a suitable pedagogy (child learning) or andragogy (adult learning) and will provide model curricula in respective branches for Universities and institutions to adopt.

Number of Courses

In the first instance, upto 247 MOOCs as under are expected to be launched by the six National MOOCs Coordinators (NMCs): NPTEL, UGC, CEC, IGNOU, NCERT, NIOS.

The SWAYAM shall also cover Skill-based courses, which cover both post-higher secondary school skills that are presently the domain of polytechnics as well as industrial skills certified by the sector skill councils of various Ministries.

Guidelines for the Preparation of MOOCS

The Ministry vide notification dated 11th March 2016 has issued 'Guidelines for Development and Implementation of Massive Open Online Courses (MOOCs)', that instructs on the: Definitions; Engagement of National Coordinators; Scope of SWAYAM; Awarding the Courses; Process Leading to development of e-Content; Technical specification for Content Development; Responsibilities of Subject Matter Experts; Responsibilities of Multimedia Lab; Re-purposing the e-Content; Features of MOOCs Compliant e-Content; Instructional systems for Design of MOOCs; Financing the MOOCS; Quality Assurance; Intellectual Property Rights; Assessment &Certification, etc.

Availability of Funds

The Ministry provides funding for creation of MOOC: (a). fresh MOOCs Compliant e-content and (b). for repurposing e-contents to MOOCs Compliant Contents, as per the 4-quadrant approach, defined in the MOOCS Guidelines.

The PIs/SMEs are also paid honourarium, for preparation of the content and for running the Course. Besides funds are also paid for engaging Teaching Assistances, Course Reviewers, conduct of Workshops and Human, Resource Support.

Transfer of Credits

The University Grants Commission in exercise of the powers conferred by Clause (f) and (g) of sub-section (1) of Section 26 of the UGC Act 1956 (No. 3 of 1956), has in its 515 the Meeting held on 20th May, 2016 approved the Credit Framework for online learning courses through SWAYAM) Regulation, 2016. It states: The parent Institution shall give the equivalent credit weightage to the students for the credits earned through online learning courses through SWAYAM platform in the credit plan of the programme. No university shall refuse any student for credit mobility for the courses earned through MooCs. The SWAYAM shall notify to the Registrars of all the Institutions & the Institutions shall, consider through their Competent Authority, the online learning courses being offered through the SWAYAM platform; and keeping in view their academic requirements, decide upon the courses which it shall permit for credit transfer. Provided that an Institution can only allow up to 20 per cent of the total courses being offered in a particular programme in a semester through Swayam Platform.

Technical Requirement

We need an active internet connection to consume course contents and system requirement are 1) Laptop/Desktop with stable internet connection. 2) Latest flash player should be installed in your computer. 3) Operating system: Mac 105, Microsoft Windows, Android, Linux. 4) Browser: 5) Port 1935RTMP 0r Port 80 should be open.

14
Interactive Multimedia

Interactive multimedia has been called a "hybrid technology." It combines the storage and retrieval capabilities of computer database technology with advanced tools for viewing and manipulating these materials. Multimedia has a lot of different connotations, and definitions vary depending on the context. In the context of upper secondary and post-secondary education, interactive multimedia is defined by three criteria:

- Interactive Multimedia is any package of materials that includes some combination of texts, graphics, still images, animation, video, and audio;
- These materials are packaged, integrated, and linked together in some way that offers users the ability to browse, navigate and analyze these materials through various searching and indexing features, as well as the capacity to annotate or personalize these materials;
- Interactive multimedia is always "reader-centered." In interactive multimedia, the reader contols the experience of reading the material by being able to select among multiple choices, choosing unique paths and sequences through the materials. One of the key features of interactive multimedia is the ability to navigate through material in whatever ways are most meaningful for individual users.

Interactive multimedia is synonymous with another frequently used term: hypermedia. Hypermedia is the multimedia version of the term hypertext. A hypertext is defined as any non-sequential, electronic text, assembled not as a seamless sequence of material with a beginning, middle and end, but as a web of interrelated chunks" of text. In a hypertext, the reader controls the sequence of reading by choosing how to navigate among these chunks of text by various electronic links.

The term "hypermedia" was coined to mean a hypertext that uses mutliple media. In other words, hypermedia is a collection of multimedia materials with multiple possible arrangements and sequences. Hypertext and hypermedia are "electronic" concepts that can only exist in a computer-based environment. Only in a computer-based environment can materials can be linked and organized in multiple ways simultaneously, and searched, sorted and navigated in hundreds of possible combinations by different users.

Imagine, for example, a large comprehensive textbook on the history of the United States. In a sense, a print version of that textbook is already "multimedia": that is, in addition to text, it might have pictures, maps, graphs, charts, timelines; furthermore, the text is made up of many different texts, being a combination of words written by the author, quotations from historical figures, perhaps commentary by other historians, and so on. But while the textbook could be thought of as a text using multiple media and materials, it is not a multimedia hypertext (or hypermedia) because, as a printed book, it can only be arranged in one order; its materials can only be accessed in the one way that the author and the publisher arranged them. True, a reader can access the print text in non-linear ways by using the index at the back of the book, or by jumping around. Still, the text itself has only one arrangement and one hierarchy of topics; and the reader's ability to navigate the materials is limited by the table of contents and the index.

Furthermore, a printed history textbook is limited by the constraints of size and practicality. Only so much information can comfortably fit between two covers of a printed book. Such practical issues have important consequences for the kinds of materials that go into the hands of readers. Limitation of size means that it is more practical to write history books that synthesize and make reference to large bodies of historical documents without being able to include very much or any of the documents, themselves—even though, for the historian, such documents are part of the vital material of history.

Now imagine a history textbook in electronic form, constructed as a work of hypermedia: how would that work be different from a printed text? First, you could fill that "book" with a far greater number of materials than you could fit between two covers of a printed book (a CD-ROM compact disk, for example, can hold the equivalent of 300,000 pages of printed material). Second, you could have a book that was truly "multimedia" in that, in addition to text, photographs, charts, and timelines, you could have audio (such as folksong recordings, famous speeches), and video (such as newsreels, film clips). Third, an electronic textbook could be constructed in an entirely different way from a printed textbook: it could have dozens of potential organizations, and thousands of internal linkages that could take the reader from one related idea to the next, in ways that would infinitely vary depending on the context of the reading experience and the interests of the reader.

Consequently, the structure of such a "text" would not be limited to the single storyline or synthesis offered by the author, but would become an intricate web of inter-relationships, something approaching the complexity of history. In discussing the transformations that ensued in turning the print version of the history book Who Built America? into a multimedia CD-ROM, editors Roy Rosenzweig and Steve Brier noted that the very nature of the "book" changed:

> The 'spine of this computer book is a basic survey of American history from 1876-1914. Added to—and in the process transforming—this textual survey are nearly two hundred 'excursions,' which branch off from the main body of the text. Those excursions contain about seven hundred source documents in various media that allow students as well as interested general readers to go beyond (and behind) the printed page and to immerse themselves in the primary and secondary sources that professional historians use to make sense of the past.

In the process of making the CD-ROM *Who Built America?*. By newly linking large amounts of inter-related materials, a print textbook became an engaging and versatile, multimedia archive of information. These new kinds of multimedia resources consequently can serve multiple purposes for many different users. Teachers could use such a text as a resource tool, gathering background information for class lectures and discovering primary documents to enrich assignments; simliarly, students, at all levels of capability, could use such a resource to begin the discovery process about historical meaning and materials.

Why use interactive multimedia?

We've seen that interactive multimedia, by definition, has the capacity to deliver large amounts of materials in multiple forms, and to deliver them in an integrated environment that allows users to control the reading and viewing experience. How then do these defining characteristics and virtues translate into benefits in an educational environment?

First of all, multimedia programmes bring to education the extraordinary storage and delivery capabilities of computerized material. This is especially important for schools, libraries, and learning institutions where books are difficult to obtain and update. Multimedia is a powerful and efficient source for acquiring learning resources. Multimedia can also provide educational institutions access to other kinds of inaccessible materials, such as hard to find historical films, rare sound recordings of famous speeches, illustrations from difficult to obtain periodicals, and so on. Multimedia can put primary and secondary source materials at the fingertips of users in even the remotest locations from major research facilities.

Secondly, it is not just sheer access to these materials that makes multimedia a powerful tool, but the control over those materials that it gives to its users. Interactive multimedia programmes enable the user to manipulate these materials through a wide variety of powerful linking, sorting, searching and annotating activities. Each of these activities can be made to reinforce and inculcate various intellectual skills, in addition to satisfying certain cognitive needs for quality learning, such as the ability to follow through links at the immediate moment when curiosity is aroused, and the ability to view different forms of the same information side-by-side.

Furthermore, interactive multimedia programmes ususally integrate some combination of orientation tools, such as timelines, graphs, glossaries, and other pedagogical guides. These kinds of tools further point to the third major benefit of multimedia: the personalization or individualization of the learning experience.

By allowing users to control the sequence and the pacing of the materials, multimedia packages facilitate greater individualization in learning, allowing students to proceed at their own pace in a tailored learning environment. Furthermore, interactive multimedia can be a powerful learning and teaching tool because it engages multiple senses. Students using multimedia are reading, seeing, hearing, and actively manipulating materials. As one educator enthusiastically put it,

> As humans, we seem hard-wired for multiple input. Consider that we remember only about 10 per cent of what we read; 20 per cent, if we hear it; %30, if we can see visuals related to what we're hearing; %50, if we watch someone do something while explaining it; but almost 90 per cent, if we do the job ourselves--if only as a simulation. In other words, interactive multimedia—properly developed and properly implemented--could revolutionize education.

Although "revolutionize" may be a bit optimistic, interactive multimedia is a promising medium for reinforcing, extending, and "supplementing" what goes on in the classroom with print materials, lectures and classroom discussions.

What Kinds of Multimedia are Available?

Educational multimedia packages and programmes come in the same range and variety as printed textbooks, and all other teaching and reference materials. Some multimedia programmes are broad and comprehensive; some are more focused. Some programmes address themselves to introductory students in a particular subject; some are suitable for more advanced students, or for teachers and scholars, or for the general public; and some work well at all ends of the spectrum depending how they are used. Similarly, some multimedia packages are more focussed on primary texts and their contexts, while others are designed to bring the user into some kind of sophisticated contact with many different kinds of materials and processes.

There are a lot of different, viable ways to categorize the different kinds of multimedia packages that are currently available. Following five categories are significant:

(I) Educational Packages: General and Comprehensive History

These are coursware packages with broad coverage, both in terms of chronology and comprehensiveness of content. These packages contain extensive print and graphic materials, as well as (usually) audio and video materials. In this category, which includes a programme, such as Who Built America?, the rationale of the design is to create a rich information environment that can either serve as a supplementary "curriculum" to a variety of historical and cultural courses, or as an informative, stand-alone research environment for teachers, scholars and the general public. These programmes often come in school and library editions, and are often keyed to printed texts.

(II) Educational Package: Focussed Topics & Collections

These educational packages are similar to those in category (I), but with particular themes or disciplinary focus. These programmes can function as either teaching or reference tools on particular topics. Two examples of programmes in this category include American Poetry: The Nineteenth Century and Origins of the Constitution. This is the broadest and most inclusive of the categories and consequently, programmes falling into this type vary quite widely in depth and quality of design.

(III) Historical Simulations

These are educational packages designed as computer-based simulations or role playing exercises. Simulations are far more common at the lower grade levels than at the college level. It is likely that this will become an increasingly popular kind of programme for higher learning levels because these programmes particularly exploit the capabilities of computing technology to calculate variables and simulate possible scenarios. SimCity, for example, is a very sophisticated simulation programme for urban planning that has been around for a relatively long time. In this Bibliography, The Election of 1912 is described as an example of an historical simulation. The incorporation of simulation exercises into classroom teaching significantly affects the dynamics of the classroom, as it re-centre the focus of classroom teaching away from the teacher and the printed text toward collaborative group work among students, focussed around contingent problems of decision-making and hypothesis testing.

(IV) Electronic Texts

In the broadest terms, electronic texts are primary literary, historical and cultural texts in electronic form, loaded into a software environment with search and analysis capabilities, and sometimes, with multimedia linking. There are currently several different kinds of electronic text packages available on the market. One kind of electronic text, such as Voyager's Expanded Book series, presents text literally as electronic "books," with a printed page-like design, and with search and annotation functions. A different kind of electronic text is IBM's Illuminated Books, containing well-known primary texts in multimedia packages with a rich assortment of pre-linked contextual and background material. Still yet a third kind of text, distributed in what is known as WordCruncher software, is neither multimedia nor hypertext, but offers large amounts of primary texts inside software capable of very powerful and complex search and indexing functions. All of the various kinds of electronic texts lend themselves to a range of teaching and research activities.

(V) Interactive Educational Reference Tools

These are educational software packages and collections that function primarily as reference tools, but in the context of education and classroom teaching or library situations. A lot of different electronic tools could be considered interactive reference tools. Only a portion of these tools are interactive multimedia. For this Guide and Bibliography, interactive reference tools refer only to those packages that are primarily educational and (usually) multimedia. An example of this category is TIME Almanac 93. Other kinds of interactive reference tools include geographic and demographic programmes, multimedia newspaper databases, and so on.

Naturally, these categories are not mutually exclusive, and in fact many multimedia programmes are characterized by more than one category. But even an imperfect categorization is helpful to begin sorting out which programmes would be most appropriate for which contexts.

Advantages of Interactive Multimedia

Interactive Multimedia has the following advantages:

I. It ensures flexible learning. Flexibility is recognized in the level of access to course; the points of entry to; and exit from courses; the place, time and pace of study; the form and pattern of interaction among learners, teachers and resources; the type and variety of resources to support study and communication; the goals or outcomes of the educating process and the methods used to measure achievements and success.

II. The interactive nature of multimedia provides immediate and comprehensive feedback to students.

III. Learning through multimedia is an active and engaged process. "Learners are actively engaged in working at task and activities they would be used"

IV. Multimedia provides complex learning environment and which also gives students their own real control over their learning environment.

V. Multimedia programmes could be designed to mix education and entertainment i.e., "edutainment'. Such sources give continuous source for knowledge for all users.

VI. Multimedia database is most useful for narrating encyclopedia available in CD-ROM packs.

VII. Multimedia components, such as graphics, animation and sound increase the learning process through visualization.

VIII. It is easy to learn and operate.

IX. It saves time. No wastage of time in rubbing out drawing and writing on the black board.

X. Graphs and diagrams can be reproduced perfectly with out changing originality.

XI. Animation in diagrams facilitates quick understanding.

XII. The rage of instructional and informational supports in teaching and learning through multimedia is very high and effective.

XIII. Using video, sound, animation, graphics, and text coupled with interactivity accelerated the learning curve of students.

XIV. Interactive Multimedia enhancing learning as well as improving the quality of education. It can be used to develop active and mastery learning.

XV. Interactive Multimedia can stimulate the student's mind and encourage learning through all senses because it can combine so many media.

XVI. Interactive Multimedia System which presents, stores, retrieves, and transmits audio, video, graphic, and textual information. These kinds of systems can have a powerful impact on the learner's problem solving abilities which can generate a positive effect.

How can multimedia be incorporated into Educational Contexts?

Rather than initially considering how a specific multimedia programme could be incorporated into a particular course, it may be more useful to think about how a shared multimedia resource collection, of multiple programmes, can be used by different institutional constituencies in different ways.

Below are listed five hypothetical scenarios and possible uses for the integration of multimedia materials into educational contexts.

Use Scenario 1: Building a Library-Based Multimedia Resource for Teachers

Before even considering the idea of implementing interactive multimedia in the classroom, for students, consider the productive use of multimedia as an efficient and effective resource for teachers. This scenario requires only a single multimedia station, placed in a library or a teachers' resource centre, with a core of multimedia programmes available.

As a teachers' resource, a solid multimedia collection can be used in a variety of valuable ways. Most directly, it can be a resource for teachers who are gathering background and contextual material for their courses. With multimedia resources, teachers can efficiently research and design lectures and assignments, as well as generate ideas and texts for clusters of materials. Because of the rich, integrative nature of the best interactive programmes, multimedia can also offer teachers provocative resources for curricular design, modelling dynamic ways that knowledge can be constructed and portrayed. This can be a valuable tool both for teachers preparing their classes, as well as teachers in training.

Mutlimedia can also serve as a teachers' resource by providing a tool for enhancing lecture and classroom presentations. An LCD (Liquid Crystal Display) that works in conjunction with a standard overhead projector allows the lecturer to project what is on the computer screen. The "resource collection" feature in the programme Who Built America? or many of the annotation features in the Voyager or IBM's electronic books are particularly conducive to this kind of presentation.

Use Scenario 2: Building a Library-Based Multimedia Resource for Students

The library-based multimedia resource that you build for students can be, of course, the same resource that is being used by teachers for the purposes outlined in the first scenario. But with some what different uses. A library-based, interactive multimedia resource complements the other collections in a library. In addition to interactive reference tools, multimedia programmes, such as electronic texts, as well as general and focused educational packages, can provide valuable enhancements to the library collection. Even before teachers begin incorporating the use of multimedia into classroom contexts, their students can begin using library-based multimedia for research papers and writing assignments, or as tools in preparing for examinations, or even for pleasure and curiosity.

Use Scenario 3: Using Multimedia Texts as Supplementary Curricular Materials for Particular Courses

Once a foundational multimedia resource collection exists in an institution—either in a library or some kind of resource centre-teachers can begin considering ways to incorporate multimedia resources into teaching. This kind of incorporation can occur at all levels of intensity and centrality. The level of impact that necessitates the least amount of revision in teaching style and classroom materials is the implementation of multimedia as a supplementary curriculum to the one covered in class. In this scenario, students are using multimedia programmes to extend discussions and assignments in class on an informal basis.

At low levels of integration, teachers can ask students to use multimedia as one of their resources for doing supplemental research to topics and texts covered in class. That is, putting in "lab" time at the multimedia station in order to augment an understanding of regular readings. At higher levels of coordination, a teacher might key particular class assignments to particular sections of multimedia packages, giving students broad reading questions that they must answer using mutlimedia resources. Or, at an even higher level of coordination, teachers might choose texts that are keyed to multimedia programmes, such as general history programmes like Who Built America? and American Impressions, or use electronic texts for research and analysis. This latter usage is explained more in scenario 4.

Use Scenario 4: Using Electronic Texts as Tools for Teaching and Reinforcing Analytic and Reading Skills

Electronic texts packages are excellent resources for teaching students a wide variety of "literacy" skills, from reinforcing reading skills (particularly in second languages) to more complicated analytic skills. Electronic texts and electronic books easily lend themselves to supplementing classroom activity when teachers key the texts they teach to electronic texts available in multimedia packages. Some of the uses that students can make of electronic book programmes include: strengthening a second reading of a text with searching and marking features;

doing search and analysis work in preparation for writing papers on texts or preparing for exams; and preparing student-led class presentations on particular texts or subjects.

Teachers can also work with students, using electronic texts, to reinforce close reading skills, using search and find functions to trace thematic and formal patterns in literature, or to engage in rhetorical analysis of sophisticated political and philosophical documents. Electronic texts can also be a useful presentation tool for instructors to use in class to focus lectures or class discussion on particular passages, or to compare similar passages by placing them side by side on the screen.

Use Scenario 5: Orienting an Entire Course Around the Use and Creation of Multimedia Materials

The most fully integrated level of using multimedia is to build an entire course around the use, and perhaps the creation, of multimedia materials. As multimedia packages become more common, some teachers are looking to multimedia as a major structuring device for their classes. It is at this level of integration that one would consider using an historical simulation, structuring at least a whole unit, if not a whole course, around the materials provided in an information-rich multimedia package.

Usually, a historical simulation would stand at the center of the course or unit, with supplementary materials surrounding it. Teachers who use historical simulations or other kinds of multimedia as the centre of their courses are usually very "activity" oriented, decentring themselves from the learning process in favour of letting students, individually or in groups, engage in elaborate exercises of discovery and creation. This kind of teaching (and learning) is not for everyone. But for those who engage in it, there is a level of involvement by students that is difficult to match through any other technique.

Conclusion

Interactive Multimedia can be used to develop active and mastery learning. In this learning situation, there is active participation on the part of the learner as opposed to passive learning, listening to lectures and demonstrations. It can stimulate the students' mind and encourage learning through all sense because multimedia can combine so many media together.

Psychologists acknowledge the important of interactive process for knowledge retention.

Interactive Multimedia generates a lot of excitement as a learning tool. It crosses traditional boundaries of school, workplace, and home, and enabling learners to choose their learning materials, in their own time and at their own pace.

15
E-Books and E-Journals

An electronic book, also known as an e-book or eBook, is a book publication made available in digital form, consisting of text, images, or both, readable on the flat-panel display of computers or other electronic devices. Although sometimes defined as "an electronic version of a printed book, some e-books exist without a printed equivalent. E-books can be read on dedicated e-reader devices, but also on any computer device that features a controllable Viewing screen, including desktop computers, laptops, tablets and Smartphones.

In the 2000s, there was a trend of print and e-books sales moving to the Internet, where readers buy traditional paper books and e-books on websites using e-commerce systems. With print books, readers are increasingly browsing through images of the covers of books on publisher or bookstore websites and selecting and ordering titles online; the paper books are then delivered to the reader by mail or another delivery service. With e-books, users can browse through titles online, and then when they select and order titles, the e-book can be sent to them online or the user can download the e-book.

The main reasons for people buying e-books online are possibly lower prices, increased comfort (as they can buy from home or on the go with mobile devices) and a larger selection of titles With e-books, electronic bookmarks make referencing easier, and e-book readers may allow the user to annotate pages. "Although fiction and non-fiction e-books formats n e-book formats, technical material is especially suited for e-book delivery because it can be [electronically] searched" for keywords. In addition, for programming books, code, examples can be copied.

Advantages

In the space that a comparably sized physical book takes up, an e-reader can contain thousands of e-books, limited only by its memory capacity. Depending on the device, an e-book may be readable in low light or even total darkness. Many e-readers have a built-in light source, can enlarge or change fonts, use text-to-speech software to read the text aloud for visually impaired, elderly or dyslexic people or just for convenience. Additionally, e-readers allow readers to look up words or find more information about the topic immediately using an online dictionary Amazon reports that 85 per cent of its e-book readers look up a word while reading.

Printed books use three times more raw materials and 78 times more water to produce when compared to e-book while e-reader costs more than most individual books, e-books may have a lower cost than paper books. E-books may be printed for less than the price of traditional books using on-demand book printers. Moreover, numerous e-books are available online free of charge on sites, such as Project Gutenberg, for example, all books printedbefore1923 are in the public domain in the United States, which enables websites to host e-book versions of such titles for free.

Depending on possible digital rights management, e-books (unlike physical books) can be backed up and recovered in the case of loss or damage to the device on which they are stored, a new copy can be downloaded without incurring an additional cost from the distributor, as well as being able to synchronize the reading location, highlights and bookmarks across several devices.

Formats

Writers and publishers have many formats to choose from when publishing e-books. Each format has advantages and disadvantages. The most popular e-readers and their natively supported formats are shown below:

Reader	*Native e-book formats*
Amazon Kindle and Fire tablets	*AZW, AZW3, KF8, non-DRM MOBI, PDF, PRC, TX T*
Barnes & Noble Nook and Nook Tablet	EPUB PDF
Apple iPad	EPUB, IBA (Multitouch books made via Books Author), PDF
Sony Reader	EPUB, PDF, TXT, RTF, DOC, BBeB
Kobo eReader and Kobo Arc	E PUPBD, TFX, TR, T HF, TMCLB, (comic), CBZ (comic)
Pocket Book Reader and Pocketbook Touch	EPUB DRM, EPUB, PDF DRM, PDF, F82, ZIP, FB2, TXT, DJVU, HTM, HTML, DOC, DOCX, RTF, CHM, TCR, PRC (MOBI)

An electronic device used to read E-Books:

- Dedicated
- Handheld
- Desktop
- ***Downloadable E-Books***: The contents of a book are available on a Website for downloading to the user's PC.
- ***Dedicated E-Book readers:*** The book's contents are downloaded to a dedicated hardware device which has a high-quality screen and special capabilities for book reading.
- ***Web-accessible E-Books***: The E-Book remains on the provider's Web site and can be accessed for a fee. Readers can 'purchase' the-books to receive indefinite access.

- ***Print-on-demand books***: The contents of a book are stored in a system connected to a high-speed, high-quality printer, from which printed and bound copies are produced on demand. The contents may be available on a chapter-by-chapter basis to enable the creation of single copies of customized books.

E-Book Challenge

How are libraries going to integrate E-Books into their services?

- Libraries circulate E-Book readers with a number of titles pre-loaded
- E-Books have records included in the catalogue
- The only E-Books available are those installed on the circulating E-Book readers
- Limited choice for users, one users unable to read library's E-Books on their own e--book readers
- Can be downloaded directly from the library catalogue to user's preferred E-Book reader
- Only one user, at one time to each purchased copy of the E-Book
- Books removed automatically from user's E-Book reader at the end of loan period and made instantaneously available in the catalogue again.
- Existing book suppliers expand services to include e-books
- New organisations manage e-book access and acquisition on behalf of the library.
- Access through passwords and authentication procedures

Internet accessible micro payments-per page view

E-Books in Distance Education

E-books have potential in enhancing distance education. In particular, e-books are able to enhance the interaction between educators and students when dealing with teaching and learning materials. To demonstrate this idea, we used a remote testing approach and asked a group of students (representative users) who had no prior e-book reading and building experience to submit assignments (typical students tasks) in LIT format. Remote testing is used when researchers are separated in space and/or time from the participants. This means that the researchers cannot observe the testing process directly and that the participants are usually not in a formal usability laboratory. On completion of the tasks, the participants were asked to describe their experiences in written form.

The task instructions were delivered with a set of lecture notes, which was also in LIT format Students were instructed to download Microsoft Reader into their personal computers and read the lecture notes containing information on how to use Microsoft Reader, the assignments, how to build an e-book from their completed assignments and how to submit it to the lecturer. They were also asked to treat the notes as if they were reading a printed version. The completed assignments were read and marked by the lecturer using Microsoft Reader as well.

The annotating, drawing and highlighting features in the reader were used extensively by the lecturer. Marked assignments containing the lecturer's annotations and comments were sent back to the students. At the end of the experiment, their experiences were noted, paying particular attention to positive and negative comments.

Positive Comments

1. Improves on-screen reading experience when compared to lecture notes sent in word processor format or slide presentation or Web pages.
2. The possibility of imitating actions used on printed notes, such as highlighting, bookmarking and annotating, is seen as very useful and helpful.
3. Accessing links from within the notes is very useful improves presentation.
4. Compiling an assignment in an e-book format, with a cover and table of contents.
5. Students could store their collections of assignments (in the e-book form) in the personalised digital library provided in the reader, thus saving physical space as well as increasing the portability.
6. By the end of their course, many e-books would have been created, thus improving the electronic authoring experience and promoting self-publishing.
7. Lecturers' comments (in digitised hand writing form and attached notes) included in the marked assignment give students a "sense of the lecturers' personal touch" on their work. In addition, students could read and identify the strengths and weaknesses of their work, from the lecturer's point of view. This "personalised" touch is one of the traditional interaction methods in the education environment, but is either difficult or not possible in other submission-return methods for electronic assignments.
8. Lecturers' responses and comments on students' work are delivered faster via the Internet.

Negative Comments

1. Even though multimedia capabilities are not considered crucial to adult learners, the need is there, especially when complex concepts are to be explained in distance education. Currently, e-book technology (i.e. either hardware or software based readers)˜ has limited multimedia features. To overcome this now, educators could include external links or simply attach email files to the students.
2. Reading online is still not as comfortable as printed notes.

E-Books and E-Journals in Distance Education

Inspite of their disadvantages and demerits, e-publications (e-books and journals) are being slowly used in distance teaching and learning in advanced countries.

Many distance-teaching institutions in USA and Europe are offering online courses using e-book technology. Though e-book has emerged as a new way of information dissemination with its potential for use in distance education for highly mobile people, it has not yet become popular for a variety of reasons including high cost of the hardware, incompatibility of e-books from one brand to another, limited availability of e-book literature and general lack of awareness. Open E-Book Forum, the international trade and standards organisation for the e-book industry is working towards development of standards and specifications for e-book developers. Open and Distance Learning institutions can take advantage of this new technology to provide easy and wide access to learning resources by transforming and/or developing lessons suitable for use in PDAs (Portable Digital Assistants). PDAs offer simple, quick and smart ways to communicate teach and learn, wherever one goes. With a PDA, a lecturer, student or administrator can do amazing things. Accessing the internet wirelessly, take notes, calculate, sketch ideas, collect data, access resources, manage activities and courses and instantly beam information to others. In 2001, the University of South Dakota in USA distributed palm hand held devices to, all of its first year undergraduate students. The PDAs normally run on a window-based operating system (OS) or Palm OS. Microsoft launched latest OS for PDAs as pocket PC 2002 in 2001.

E-Journals

Of late several e-journals are emerging in education and distance education. Glasgow University Library listed (www.lib.ga.ac.uk) 220 e-journals in education, distance education and related areas. It is interesting to note that several of these are free journals. The important free e-journals are listed in Annexure II.

The use of e-journals is on the increase although this new development has not yet fully adopted by the policy-makers and innovators in distance education even in the developed countries. To be adopted, e-journals should perform the same function as their predecessors, the print journals, such as building a collective knowledge base, communicating information, validating the quality of research and building distance education communities.

Building on the tradition of print journals, the e-journals can be a forum where scholars articulate their needs' by writing, editing, and refereeing articles that evaluate and contextualize important resources. Scholars so these in print journals as well, but in an electronic format the resources can be hyperlinked and thus, immediately integrated for the readers. With the help of Internet technology and website management, users can easily get the paper by searching by author, keyword, title, journal, year, and publication format. Search results can be viewed on the screen, or they can be mailed to the user directly formats; plain text, Bib Tex, or HTML.

But, the online journals do not have the credibility of traditional journals. Because print journals have built their reputation by publishing some classic theoretical, scientific and technical papers, and because the quality and reputation of print journals are based on the standards maintained by the editorial boards, people usually think famous print journals receive more respect and are of higher quality. Thus, more and more papers are submitted to print journals. Reputation is based on good papers and good papers make the reputation ever better. That's the reason why people trust and like print journals. The same situation will happen to the electronic journals. However, due to the short history, online journals haven't established their reputation yet.

E-Books in India: The Present and Future

With the launch of Amazon bundle in India, clearly e-books for the first time are getting attention by publishers as well as readers. There is a lot of speculation going one-book market in India. Someone is saying that it will pick like ecommerce has picked up.

EBooks phenomenon has been unsuccessful in India, everyone talks of it, but no one buys it. Why? Very simple, nobody told them (readers) to buy.

Are eBooks better than printed books? In US-UK, eBooks sale more than printed books, this clearly shows eBooks are worthy.

So, who pushed/evangelized the eBook concept to readers there? Amazon, Apple, Google, Nook, Kobo, Adobe. Western people do listen to their technology companies, because they have certainly changed their lives.

So, again coming back to original question why eBook has been a flop show in India? Why nobody told the readers here to switch to eBooks?

Here is Q analysis:

- Indian Publishers don't understand technology (in fact, they hate technology. I don't know why). So they were not interested in eBooks.
- Schools/Colleges don't want their students to use eBooks. It's very new concept to them. They don't like their students to use gadgets (tablets) extensively E-learning companies can throw some light on readiness of school/college principals on use of technology.
- Governments (ministers &secretaries) don't know that eBook exists at all.
- Parents are more bothered about the marks of their kids. They want their child to remember things, not analyze things. They believe tablets are for entertainment. It's a diversion for their kids.
- Now what about readers? Why they didn't ask for eBooks? I found only reason-Readers here like the smell of printed books. I don't know what kind of spiritual smell is there, which western people don't get.

e-Book Consumption Factors

- Price of eBooks
- Push from Government/Schools/Colleges/Corporate

E-Books can't be priced in the range of printed books. It has to be at least 40-70 per cent cheaper, than the discounted price of printed books.

Many publishers argue that with the growth of e-Book their printed sales will come down and finally they will make loss. I totally disagree. Till now, publishing industry is totally dependent on distribution. Many good books have not reached to masses because of poor distribution infrastructure in India. E-Books don't have that issue.

Push from institutions is equally important. Readers want some angel to come and tell them-hey why don't you buy e-Book, it's cheaper, better and reading is more social. Your experience of reading will be much more than reading dead tree-books.

Annexure I

Websites to Download Free E-Books

1. Project Gutern berg (www.guternberg.org)
2. Open Library (www.openlibrary.org)
3. Google e Book store (www.play.google.com/store/books)
4. Amazon Free Kindle Books (www.amazon.com/b)
5. Internet Archive (www.archive.org/details/texts)
6. Many Books (www.manybooks.net)
7. BookBoon (www.bookboon.com)
8. Lib Gen/Library Genesis (www.gen.lib.rus.ec)
9. Free Book Spotn (www.freebookspot.es)
10. Free e Books (www.free-ebooks.net)
11. Ebook Bike (www.ebook.bike)
12. Issue (www.issue.com)
13. Librivox (www.librivox.org)
14. Get Free E Books (www.get freebooks.com)
15. Free Computer Books (www.freecomputerbooks.com)
16. Baen (www.baen.com)
17. Books Pics (www.bookspics.com)
18. Free Tech Books (www.freetechbooks.com)
19. Open Library (www.openlibrary.org)
20. Know Free (www.knowfree.tradepub.com)
21. Open Culture (www.openculture.com/free ebooks)
22. Online Programming Books (www.onlineprogrammingbooks.com)
23. Learn Pub (www.learnpub.com)
24. Snip Files (www.snipfiles.com)
25. Biblio stastic (www.bibliotastic.com)
26. Book Yards (www.bookyards.com)
27. Free Books (www.freebooks.com/publications)
28. The Online Books Page (www.digitallibrary.upenn.edu/books)
29. e Book Lobby (www.ebooklobby.com)
30. My anonamouse (www.myanonamouse.net/login)
31. Avax Home (www.avxhome.in/ebooks)
32. O' Really (www.oreilly.com)

Annexure II

Important Free Journal

The AASA Professor:
http://www.aasa.org/puiblications/tap/index.htm
Academe:
http//lwww.aaup.org/publications/Academe/
Academic Leadership:
http//www.academicleadershiporgl
Australian Education Computing:
http://www.ascilite.org.au/ajet/ajet.htms
Canadian Journal of Education Administration and Policy:
http://www.umanitoba.ca/publications/cjeap/

Canadian Journal of Learning and Technology:
http://www.cjit.ca
Converge:
http://www.centerdigitaled.com/converge/
Current Issues in Education:
http://www.cie.asu.edu/index.html
Education Policy Analysis Archives:
http://www.epaa.asu.edu
Educational Researcher:
http://www.aera.net/publisher/
Educational Technology and Society:
http://www.ifets.ieee.org/periodocal/
Electronic Journal of Science Education:
http://www.eastern.edu/publications/emme/
Interactive Multimedia Electronic Journal of Computer-Enhanced Learning:
http://www.imej.wfu.edu/
International Education Journal:
http://www.ed.sturt.flindersedu.au/iej/
International Review of Research in Open and Distance Learning:
http://www.irrodl.org/
Journal of Career and Technical Education:
http://www.scholar.lib.vt.edu/ejournals/JCTE/
Journal of Educational Enquiry:
http://www.education.unisa.edu.au/JEE/
Journal of Interactive Media in Education:
http://www-jime.open.ac.uk/
Journal of Research for Educational Leaders:
http://www.uiowa.edu/jrel/
Journal of Scholarship of Teaching and Learning:
http://jset.univ.edu
Networks: An On-line Journal for Teacher Research:
http://www.oise.utoronto.ca/ctd/networks/
New Horizons for Learning Online Journal:
https/lwww.newhorizons.org/journal/newjournal.htm
Practical Assessment, Research and Evaluation:
http/ledresearch.org/pare/Home.htm
T.H.E. Journal:
http://www.thejournal.com/
Teacher Magazine:
http://www.teachermagazine.org
Training Journal:
http://www.trainingjournal.com/
Turkish Online Journal of Distance Education
http://www.tojde.anadolu.edu.tr/

Appendix

Apex Educational Bodies in India

- BARC-Bhabha Atomic Research Centre
  BARC offers rewarding career opportunities to young qualified people in the areas of Nuclear Science and Technology. Chosen aspirants can pursue innovative research in Physics, Chemistry, Geology, Geophysics, Engineering and Biosciences at the centre.
- AICTE-All India Council for Technical Education
  AICTE, a national-level council for technical education. It governs the Boards of Architecture, Hotel Management and Catering Technology, Information Technology, Post Graduate Education and Research in Engineering and Technology, Undergraduate Studies in Engineering etc.
- AIMA-All India Management Association
  AIMA carries out a range of management related activities and initiatives, such as Distance Management Education, Management Development Programmes, Research and Publications, Testing Services, and National events and competitions.
- BCI-Bar Council of India
  BCI promotes and sets standards for legal education and grants recognition to Universities whose degree in law will serve as qualification for enrollment as a lawyer. BCI founded the National Law School of India University for research and instruction of law.
- CDAC-Centre for Development of Advanced Computing
  CDAC carries out R & D work in design, development and deployment of advanced information technology based solution. It offers advanced computing and software development courses in Software technologies, VLSI designs, Digital Multimedia, etc.
- CHD-Central Hindi Directorate
  CHD conducts correspondence courses for teaching Hindi language to non-Hindi speaking Indians and
- CIAE-Central Institute of Agricultural Engineering
  CIAE in Bhopal is a nodal institute in India conducts research and development to facilitate agricultural mechanization and conservation of soil and water. It offers course in Energy in Agriculture at the M Tech level.
- CIET-Central Institute of Educational Technology
  CIET provides and promotes educational technology especially at the school level. It publicizes alternative learning systems. Directs and coordinates the academic and technical programmers of SIET.
- CIEFL-Central Institute of English and Foreign Languages

CIEFL is a National Institute for providing higher education in English and other Foreign Languages in India. It conducts various Post Graduate and Research programmes. CIEFL has three campuses—Hyderabad, Lucknow and Shillong.

- CIIL-Central Institute of Indian Languages
  CIIL strives to maintain the unity of Indian languages through scientific studies. It governs five centres, such as School of Applied Language Sciences and Technology, School of Literary, Cultural and Translation Studies, School of Classical Languages, etc.
- Central Library, IIT Madras
  The Central Library is well-equipped with all modern facilities and resources in the form of CD-ROM, On-line databases, microfiche, microfilms, audio-video cassettes, books, journals, standards, specifications, thesis, reports, etc.
- CISCE-Council for Indian School Certificate Examinations
  CISCE develops effective teaching-learning provisions. Its main function is to conduct Indian School Certificate Examinations, The Indian School Certificate, and the Certificate in Vocational Education.
- CSTT-Commission of Scientific and Technical Terminology
  CSST works for the development of uniform technology for Hindi and other modern Indian languages. It is involved in development of language technology for books and periodicals at all the educational levels-primary and higher education besides University level.
- COA-Council of Architecture
  COA is responsible for regulating the education and practice of profession throughout India besides maintaining the register of Architects. Any person willing to pursue 'Architecture' as a profession will have to register with the Council of Architecture.
- CSIR-Council of Scientific and Industrial Research
  CSIR'S objective is todevelop new tools and applications for the industrial segment of the country and to accelerate the scientific and technological progress of the country.
- DCI-Dental Council of India
  DCI, a statutory body has representatives of the Central Government, State Government, Universities, Dental Colleges, Medical Council of India and the Private Practitioners of Dentistry. It was constituted with a view to regulate the dental education, dental profession and dental ethics.
- DOEACC-Department of Electronics Accreditation of Computer Courses
  The courses of DOEACC commence from Certificate Level and goes up to Masters level. The society also offers horizontal level entry at higher level. In the scheme, not only can students enroll but working too.
- DTE Maharashtra-Directorate of Technical Education

DTE Maharashtra manages and directs technical institutes-engineering colleges, polytechnics, industrial training institutes, and technical high schools of the state. The directorate has to ensure that a candidate gets the right sort of professional training in his/her chosen discipline which must meet to modern Industry demands.

- FTTI-Film and Television Institute of India
  Film and Television Institute of India (FTTI), National School of Drama (NSD), Satyajit Ray Film and Television Institute (SRFTI), and Shri Ram Centre for Performing Arts (SRCPA) are the apex institutes under films and dramatics.
- ICPR-Indian Council of Philosophical Research
  The main objectives of ICPR are to establish, administer and manage the Indian Council of Philosophical Research. The Governing Body (GB) and the Research Project Committee (RPC) are the main authorities of the Council.
- IIAS-Indian Institute of Advanced Study
  IIAS is a residential centre for research and encourages promotion of creative thought in areas which have deep human significance, and provides an environment suitable for academic research.
- IIFT-Indian Institute of Foreign Trade
  IIFT has evolved itself into a complete business school, offering Management Programmes in various streams of International Business. Besides, offering full time programmes in Management, it also offers part-time programmes for working professionals.
- IISc-Indian Institute of Science
  IISc is a leading institution of research and advanced instruction. Besides offering formal education the institute also offers short-term programmes for engineers and scientists. The Continuing Education Programme of the institute covers a wide range of topics.
- ISRO-Indian Space Research Organisation
  The objective of ISRO is to develop space technology and its application to various national activities. ISRO has operationalised two major satellite systems, namely Indian National Satellites (INSAT) and Indian Remote Sensing.
- ISI-Indian Statistical Institute
  ISI is well-equipped for imparting teaching and training of mathematics, statistics and allied disciplines. The institute now comprises over 250 faculty members and over 1,000 supporting staff and several modern-day gadgets.
- IGNOU-Indira Gandhi National Open University
  IGNOU delivers quality higher education, in various disciplines, through distance mode. 35 countries are the takers of its undergraduate, postgraduate and certificate programmes.

- IPR-Institute for Plasma Research
  The plasma research activities of IPR institute includes, Studies on high temperature magnetically confined plasmas, Basic experiments in plasma physics, and Industrial plasma processing and application.
- ICAI-Institute of Chartered Accountants of India
  ICAI is contributing towards education, professional development, and maintenance of high accounting, auditing and ethical standards.
- ICSI-Institute of Company Secretaries of India
  ICSI develops and regulates the profession of company secretaries. It is the ONLY institute which offers this course and awards the certificate bestowing the designation of company secretary to qualifying members of the institute.
- IEG-Institute of Economic Growth
  IEG is recognized as one of the leading research institute in the areas of economics and social development. It broadly focusses on Agriculture and rural development, Environment and resource economics, Labour and welfare, etc.
- IMSc-Institute of Mathematical Sciences
  IMSc carries out research in frontier areas of mathematics, physics and computer sciences. Research at IMSc is well-supported by Department of Atomic Energy Government of India and Government of Tamil Nadu.
- IOP-Institute of Physics
  IOP carries out research tasks in theoretical and experimental areas of High Energy, Nuclear, Atomic, Molecular and Condensed Matter Physics, etc.
- JNV-JawaharNavodayaVidyalayas
  JNV's are fully residential and co-educational schools covering classes VI to XII. Education in these Vidyalayas is free for all enrolled students including lodging, boarding, text books, uniforms, etc.
- KHS-Kendriya Hindi Sansthan
  KHS promotes the Hindi language by teaching Hindi language to the non-Hindi speaking population of our country in order to propagate it as their second language.
- MCI-Medical Council of India
  MCI sets standard of higher qualifications in medicine and recognition of medical qualifications in India and abroad. It deals with medical colleges and hospitals and medical professionals of the country.
- NAAC-National Assessment and Accreditation Council
  NAAC certifies institutions of higher learning (Colleges, Universities, Institutes, etc.) in the country but, it does not include the institutes providing technical education.
- NBA-National Board of Accreditation
  NBA conducts periodical evaluation of the technical institutions and programmes on a periodical basis according to specified norms and standards as recommended by AICTE council to it.

- NCERT-National Council for Educational Research and Training
  NCERT undertakes Research, Developemental activities, and Training. It provides assistance to the government at the centre and at state levels on the academic matters.
- NCTE-National Council of Teacher Education
  NCTE sets up norms and standards for teacher's education right from pre-school teacher education to post graduate level teacher education. It plans, coordinates and implements innovative ways to educate teachers.
- NIFT-National Institute of Fashion Technology
  The Government of India established NIFT. It is acknowledged as the hallmark of Indian Fashion Industry across the country.
- NIOS-National Institute of Open Schooling
  NIOS caters to the educational needs of the children out of school, school drop-outs and socially and economical backward section of the learner population.
- NITIE-National Institute of Industrial Engineering
  NITIE teaches materials management, work studies, inventory control, shop floor management and personnel management to India's industry professionals.
- NLM-National Literacy Mission
  NLM was established to make everyone self-reliant in reading, writing and arithmetic, and to make them aware of the development issues affecting the society.
- NUEPA-National University of Education Planning and Administration
  NUEPA focusses on planning, management and capacity building in educational policy, through research, training, consultancy and dissemination. It has nine academic and one administrative unit.
- NVS-NavodayaVidyalaySamiti
  NVS manages co-educational residential schools known as JawaharNavodayaVidyalayas across the country, for imparting education from class VI to XII. e-education at NavodayaVidyalaya is free of cost.
- PCI-Pharmacy Council of India
  PCI prescribes, regulates and maintains minimum educational standards for the training of pharmacists uniformly in the country. Any institute providing pharmacy education in the country requires registering with Pharmacy Council of India.
- RSS-Rashtriya Sanskrit Sansthan
  RSS develops, propagates, and encourages Sanskrit learning and teaching in and around the country. It imparts various educational programmes in Sanskrit through its various affiliated institutions.
- RIT-Regional Institute of Technology
  RIT Jamshedpur is a seat of scientific & technological learning. It offers B.Sc. (Engg.) and other Postgraduate courses. NRI Admissions are also taken.

- RCI-Rehabilitation Council of India
  RCI maintains and standardizes the standard of training professionals. It has a National Programme Policy in the form of Primary Health Center and Bridge Courses.
- SPJMIR-SP Jain Institute of Management and Research
  The course curricula offered by the SPJMIR similar to top ranked business schools of the world like Harvard, etc. The institute works in close co-operation with Industrial sector and hence provides best training for its students.
- SINP-Saha Institute of Nuclear Physics
  SNIP offers a number of Research, Doctoral, and Post Doctoral Programmes in Physics and Nuclear Physics.
- SIET-State Institute of Education Technology
  SIET was established to promote quality in primary education through INSAT-1B.
- TTTI Bhopal-Technical Teacher's Training Institute
  TTTI has developed as a centre of excellence in the area of technical education. It offers postgraduate education in Technician field, along with several other related courses and projects.
- UNESCO-United Nations Educational, Scientific & Cultural Organization.
  UNESCO dealt with science and technology programmes in eleven South and Central Asian countries. Later, it also incorporated communication, education and culture programmes.
- UPSC-Union Public Service Commission
  UPSC conducts competitive examinations on all India basis for recruiting to the various posts in the fields of civil services, engineering, medical and forest service.
- UGC-University Grants Commission_
  UGC has been co-ordinating, determining and maintaining standards of university education and teaching in the country.
- VCI-Veterinary Council of India
  VCI regulates Veterinary practice and Veterinary education across the country.
- XLRI-Xavier Labour Relations Institute
  XLRI emphasizes also on fellowship and research programmes apart from training management graduates.

References

Abhishek Bhatnagar (2018). The Advent of Technology in Education in India: Opportunities and Challenges *www.youthkawaaz.com*

Abdul Latheef, N. (2018). Gateway for Teaching and Learning: Role of Swayam Prabha. *University News,* 56(47).

Agarwal, BC (2005). Educational Media in India in V. Naidou & H. Remzy (eds) *Educational Media in Asia.* Vancouver, Canada.

Aman deep Kaur (2019). Digital Education: Scope and Challenges. *International Journal of Applied Research,* SP4.

Amit Prakash, Anjali Karol Mohan and Bidisha Chaudhuri (2019). What do Citizens value in E-Governance. *Economical and Political Weekly.* LIV No. 10.

Anoop Swaroop (2018). Digital Initiatives in Higher Education. *Indian Didactic Association.*

Anup Kumar (2014). Open Educational Resources: Policy Perspectives and National Initiatives. *Science and Technology, (3).*

Anderieen Diana Phillimis (2019). Smartphones Round the Clock. *University News,* 57 (18).

Arulsamy, S and Sivakumar, P (2004). Interactive Multimedia in Technology and Learning. *University News,* 42 (30).

Armelini, A and Padilli Rodriguez, BC (2018). Are Moocs Pedagogically Innovative? *Journal of Interactive Online Learning,* 14 (1).

Blended Learning—The Future of Upskilling and Reskilling in Digital India. *www.iiht.com*

Blended Learning—The Best of Online and Campus University Education. *www.distancelearningportal.com*

Denial Fernandes, SJ (2019). Moocs in Higher Education: Opportunity or Challenges? *University News,* 57(18).

Dennis Frezzo (2017). The Role of Technology in the Education of the Future. *World Economic Forum.*

Commission Of the European Communities (2008). *The use of ICT to support innovation and lifelong learning for all—a report on Progress.* Bruseels: European Commission.

Conway, MH (2000). Economic of Online Journals. *Science Editor,* 23(2).

Capper, J. and Copple (1985). *Computer Use in Education: Research Review and Instructional Implications.* Washington DC: Centre for Research and Practice.

Ekta Srinivastava and Nisha Agarwal (2013). E-Learning New Trend in Education and Training. *International Journal of Advance Reserch,* 1(18).

Five big changes every classrooms will need for the new era of education. *India Today Web Desk,* 10-1-2019.

Gangadhara Chary (2016). Essentiality of E-Learning to the Learning Countries. *International Journal of Innovative Research in Advanced Engineering.* 12(3).

Hawkins, D (2000). Electronis Books: A Major Publisjing Revolution. *Online,* 15(28).

How the Indian Government is taking Education to the Masses using Technology and Internet (2016). *Scoop News.*

Indrajeet Datta (2016). OER Oppertunities and Challenges for Indian Higher Education. *Turkish Online Journal of Distance Education, 17*(2).

Jaya Prakash and Venkataramana R (2006). Role of Digital Libraries in E-Learning. *Gandhalaya Saraswarm,* April.

Joshi, A (2012) A Technique in Teaching Process in the Classroom. *Current World Environment,* 7(23).

Kessler, Sarah (2010). Eight Technology is Improving Education, *www.mashable.com*

Kumar, A. and Tiwari (2011). A comparative Studt of the Effectiveness of CAI Programmes and Traditional Methodds of Teaching. *International Reforred Research Journal,* Vol-3 (27).

KPMG in India and Google (2017). *Online Education in India:2021.*

Ligi, B and William Dharma Raja (2012). Mobile Learning in Higher Education. *International Journal of Research,* 5(4).

Manoj Yanam (2019) A Panacea for Indian Education. *Careers 360,* April, 2019.

Mason, R (1994). *Using Communications Media in Open and Flexible Learning.* London: Kogan Page.

Manjunath, BR (2018). Technology: Boon or Blame. *University News.* 56(35).

Michael Lorenzen (1998). Distance education: Delivering Instruction in cyberspace *C&R News. 59*(3).

Misra, PR (2009). *ODL Technologies for Lifelong Learning in India: Possibilities and Strategies.* MJPR University.

Misra, S and Sharma, RC (2005). Developing of E-Learning in India. *University News,* 43(11).

Minal Anand 5 Reasons Why Digitalisation is a must for Education Sector: *www.enterpreneur.com*

MHRD (2015). *Guidelines for Development and Implementation of Moocs. Government of India.*

MHRD, Govt of India (2017). Technology Enable Learning. *www.mhrd.gov.in technology-enable-learning*

Mounissamy and Kaliamml (2005). Access of E-Journals in the Institutions of Higher Technical Education through INDEST Consortium. *University News,* 43(07).

Mohanty, J (2004). *Modern Trends in Indian Education.* New Delhi: Deep & Deep.

Naushad Kabir, SK and Sampita Das (2019). Scneario of Moocs Practices in Indian Higher Educational System: A Government Initiative. *University News,* 56(53).

Narula, TK and Sadhana, R (2017). *International Journal on Emerging Technologies,* 8(1).

Naidu, S (2003). *E-Learning: A Guide of Principles, Procedures and Practices.* New Delhi: CEMCA-COL.

National Digital Library of India. www.ndl.gov.in

Needs and Importance of ICT in Education. www.myclassboard.com

Nivedhita Jha and Veena Shenoy (2016). Digitisation of Indian Education Process. A hope or Hype. *Journal of Business and Managents,* 18(10).

Prensky, M (2008). The Role of Technology in Teaching and the Classroom. *Education Technology,* Nov-Dec.

Punam Bansal (2014). Blended Learning in Indian Higher Education. *Internal Journal of Applied Research and Studies,* 3(2).

Rakesh Jain and Singh, AK (2018). Exploring the Effective Moocs Development Methodology for SWAYAM. *University News,* 56(31).

Rory Mc Greal (2017). Special Report on the Role of OER in Supporting Sustainable Development. *The International Review of Research in Open ans Distributed Learning,* 18(2).

Role of Media and Technology in Distance Education. Teaching online Net.

Sarvi, J, Dhanarajan, G and Hitendera Pilla (2015). Open Education Resources: Enhancing Education provision and Practice. *ADB Briefs.*

Satyanaranana, P and Ennamuel, Dk (2014). E-Learning in India: Initiatives and Issues. *University News,* 52(10).

Sajid Khan, M (2013). Why Blended Learning in Future of Indian Education *www.moneycontrol.com*

Sameer Babu, M. and Sarwat Ali (2018). Moocs Platforms as a Potential Genre for Progressive Professional Development of Teachers. *University News,* 56(43).

Sangetha, K Lal Manohar and Sharma, SK (2011). E-Learning as a Research Area. *International Journal of Advance Computer Science and Applications,* 2(9).

Satyanaranana, P and Emmanuel, DK (2015). Use of ICT in India's First Open University: Experinces and Perceptions of Learners. *Turkish Online Journal of Distance Education,* 16(1).

Stork, PP (2000). The Promice of e-book Publishing. *The International Writing Journal,* 4(9).

Sunil M Gawande (2019) E-Learning in Higher Education in India: Trends and Issues *University News,* 57(13).

Sundarajan, N (2019). Education for All: A Reality Through Moocs. *University News,* 57(18).

Swayam Prabha *www.swayamprabha.gov.in*

Ten Top Advantages and Disadvantages of Technology in Education (2015). *Crystal Ayes*

The Role of Technology in the Education of the Future. www.weforum.org

This is how ICT has helped in the evolution of education Industry. *India Today App Magazine,* 13-11-2018.

Tyagi, D and Mishra, K (2018). Neo-ICT and Pedagogy Symbiosis in Teacher Education Programmes for Next Generation Teachers. *University News,* 56(24).

Vijaya Kumar (2009). Open Education Research in India's National Development. *Open Learning: The Journal of Open, Distance and E-Learning.*

Vipin Saxena, Pawan Kumar Chaurasia (2015). E-learning through National Knowledge Network. *International Journal of Computer and Electronic Engineering,* 3(4).

Wilson, R (2001). Evolution of Electronic Books. *Ariadne* (29).

Index